TURNING POINT

DR ROHAN WEERASINGHE

For Stine, my inspiration and unwavering supporter

For Savannah, my beautiful bundle of joy

To my parents, thank you for your gifts of love and life

THE BALD TRUTH

A **6** Step
Process for
Transforming
Your Life

TURNING
POINT

DR ROHAN
WEERASINGHE

TURNING POINT

A 6 Step Process for Transforming Your Life

First published in 2011 by

Ecademy Press
48 St Vincent Drive, St Albans, Herts, AL1 5SJ
info@ecademy-press.com
www.ecademy-press.com

Printed and bound by Lightning Source in the UK and USA
Cover by Stine Jorgensen
Set in Myriad and Warnock by Karen Gladwell
Dr Rohan Weerasinghe portraits by Michael Inns

Printed on acid-free paper from managed forests. This book is
printed on demand, so no copies will be remaindered or pulped.

ISBN 978-1-907722-20-2

Contents

Acknowledgements

This book is the result of a long journey, spanning over 20 years since the seeds of the idea were first planted. It's been a long germination period and the timing is exactly as it is supposed to be.

One does not write a book without the support and encouragement of others. I feel blessed to have had great friends and mentors over the years who encouraged and reminded me that I have a message that others should hear. To all of those people, many of whom are not named here, I thank you from the core of my heart.

In particular, I want to thank my beautiful Stine for being there every step of the way, for your love, constant support, feedback, incredible insights and patient discussions about this book. You inspire me every day. To my mother, Helen Rettie, thank you for always being my biggest supporter; for never doubting me and for bringing us up under such difficult circumstances. Also for instilling such great values in me at an early age – thank you.

For your great friendship, for being a rock and always encouraging me and consistently reminding me, for almost a decade, that I must spread my message to the world, I want to thank Raj Deb. You are one of the shining lights on my life journey.

For the positive encouragement, thoughtful ideas, support and great feedback, I would also like to extend a warm thank-you to Corey Donoghue, Miranda Leslau, Alistair Crooks, Michael Nixon-Livy, Iain Edwards, Ajita Deb, Jane Humby, Simon Parker, Ryan Pinnick, Clinton Ratanatray, Clare Hunter, David Leon, Gill Fielding, Sabrina Antou and Sylvia Rai.

Thank you also to all those of you who responded to my pre-book questionnaire, who shared areas of their lives that they felt needed turning points.

For her great organisational skills and managing so many things during the writing of this book, I would like to thank Louise Gwilliam. For your book-writing coaching and guidance and for helping me to put my ideas into this first book, thank you Mindy Gibbins-Klein – it made all the difference.

Finally, I would like to extend a special thanks to the tens of thousands of people in my audiences and to the Clients who I have coached and mentored. Through you I have learnt, grown and been inspired. This book would not have been possible without you.

How To Use This Book Effectively

Prepare To Change

Are you ready to make some important positive changes to your life?

If the answer to this question is *YES*, then this book will provide you with the exact tools necessary to make such changes. For over 20 years I have coached and spoken in front of tens of thousands of people around the world. Over those years I have observed that no matter what age, culture, gender or race, we *all* experience times in our lives when we face personal, financial or business challenges. These specific points in our life-journey are often critical moments, turning points that can redefine how we live the rest of our lives. It is when we reach these points that we reach out and ask someone for help. That is why I am here with you in the pages of this book – to help coach you through the Change Process.

The Bald Truth provides you with a proven process that can be applied to any area of your life – no matter what your circumstances. If you engage fully and you are committed to the change that you want to make, then the impact of this process will be significant and rapid.

After earning my PhD, during my life as a Civil Engineer, I was one of the world's leading specialists in stabilising ground that collapses under buildings and then rebuilding their foundations. Combining this expertise with my vast experience in coaching and working with audiences, I have created a form of Human Engineering that anybody can use to *re-stabilise* their life and create new *life-foundations*. Ultimately what this life-technology does is enable rapid and impactful changes. This is the process you are about to learn and apply to your life.

As we go through the book, it will be as though I am sitting with you, coaching you every step of the way. I will also share with you real life stories that my clients and I have personally experienced. At each stage you will begin to notice that your thoughts become clearer and the path ahead will start to reveal itself. You will notice internal positive changes happening to your beliefs and outlook about your current and future situations. You will feel more confident in everything you do and your communication both with yourself and others will improve dramatically. Be aware that those around you will start to notice and comment on this too. Furthermore, you will find yourself naturally starting to use these tools with friends, family and even business associates. Such is the power of what this book holds for you.

There are three very important conditions that will impact your success. If you align with these at a high level of energy, then what you hold in your hands is an incredible opportunity to dramatically influence both your life and those you care about:

1. *Your desire and willingness to change*

2. *Your level of excitement about your future*

3. *The commitment and physical action you put into making these changes*

A Break-Down of the Book

Section One of the book is designed to help you clear the path ahead in order that you can experience positive changes quicker and more effectively. You will learn the four ingredients essential for creating internal change. You will also discover the seven most dangerous obstacles that can crush positive change. The final part of Section One is for me to give you a massive PROD. It is at this point that you will develop a completely different perspective on your situation and you will feel focused and decisive about your next steps. This is where you take ownership of whatever is happening in your world and we step forward together into the Six Step Change Process.

Section Two is the Six Step Change Process. This is where you will roll up your sleeves and we will work together to get to the very core of what makes you who you are, why you do what you do and how you want to redefine yourself and your life. Step 1 is where you will carry out an in-depth review of how you are communicating at a conscious and subconscious level. This is where a lot of positive and negative programming can take place. Step 2 addresses your life values –in order to live a fulfilling and purposeful life you must know what core values you want to live by. I will help you identify your existing life values and then, where necessary, completely redefine and re-order them. When done properly, this one step can completely change your view of the world. As we move to Step 3 we look at your Life Rules. Your patterns of success and failure will be a direct result of a set of Life Rules by which you live every moment. In this step you are going to completely rewrite your Life Rules. The positive impact of this will show up both on a personal and professional level.

In Step 4 we dig deeper. Many of the beliefs that you hold today are those of a child, shaped by years of external influence. In this step we will identify any restricting and damaging beliefs, clear them rapidly and then reconstruct specific elements of your belief system. This will be a very powerful and emotional process. Step 5 is about your environment. To achieve sustainable and positive change, every human being must have a supportive internal (mental/emotional) and external environment. Step 5 will involve you reviewing both of these in your current life and will involve you making changes to how you think, who you mix with and potentially where you live. Finally in Step 6 you will explore your purpose. This change process can only have true lifetime value to you if you are aligned with a bigger vision for your life. Here I will walk you through a process for helping you identify what you are passionate about so that you can wake up each day with a purpose not only for that day but also for your life.

Section Three covers the Three Pillars Of Life Balance – health, relationships and money. As I travel the world delivering seminars and working with people from all backgrounds, these are the three areas that people want to work on more than any other. This section of the book will be more like a private mentoring session with me where I will explain the fundamental tools that you must learn and apply if you wish to have more balance in each of these areas. You can increase your natural energy levels, eat healthier and feel more vibrant. You can attract an amazing partner or continue to experience a wonderful and fulfilling relationship. And yes, you can learn to manage your finances and create financial independence if you choose to. Section Three will help put you on the path to success in these three vital areas of your life.

Section Four is where the rubber meets the road. This section has one focus and that is action. It is also a call to arms and a reminder of what you must do next to keep the momentum going.

My Message To Couples

You may be reading this book now and have an urge to encourage your partner to do the same thing but they may not be at that level of development yet. Alternatively, you and your partner may be ready to make changes and are reading this together. If your partner is not on this journey with you, you may be saying "they just don't seem to want to grow or put the effort in to make changes". It may also be that your partner has joined you on this journey but they are simply not growing as quickly as you. This is a perfectly natural reaction and you are not alone. I have witnessed countless couples arguing over a decision related to their business, their finances, health or relationship. That is part of the natural cycle of any relationship – you both have different values and beliefs.

My experience has simply been to be patient. If you can allow the growth to take place in you first and don't try to force it on your partner, things will start to happen for you both. Remember that you *can't push a rope, but you can pull a rope* and so if you focus on you first, find a common vision that you both want as a couple, then you can start to lead the way for the two of you.

A Final Comment Before You Start

What I will share with you in this book is not necessarily all new information; other great teachers have also shared similar philosophies. However, what you will receive is a blend of my own personal experiences as a coach, mentor and speaker plus the tools that I have developed or adapted from my own mentors. I believe that I am a *messenger*, and each messenger on this earth has a different voice. It is my sincere hope that my message will connect with you at a deep level and in such a way that you are able to make dramatic and positive life changes.

Most importantly, if you follow the book from start to finish you will be walked through a proven process that has worked for countless people. Each stage is essential to your personal growth and for making dramatic changes in the way you think, act, feel and see the world. What is really exciting is that what you learn here can be applied across every area of your life from health to wealth and love to adventure.

So be different. Act different. Do not allow those around you who do not have the same vision as you to hold you back. Life is too short. There are too many amazing experiences that you can have *if* you are prepared to change the way you live and the way you see things. This book is *for* and *about you*.

This is not a free ride. But it will be an amazing adventure and a journey that will lead you to what I truly believe will be a path of higher consciousness. I can guarantee you this. There will be a point in the future when you look back at this moment in your life and you will be stunned by the transformation that you will have gone through. That is the power of the journey that you will go through if you read, implement and consistently apply what I am going to teach you. That is my promise.

If you are ready to come on the journey with me, take my hand and let's take the first step.

SECTION ONE

TURNING POINT

Clearing The Obstacles On Your Path

Four Ingredients That Enable Positive Change

Introduction

We must remember that change is inevitable in every area of our life. Changes occur all around us in our external environment and in many cases we have absolutely no control over of these occurrences. However, what we have incredible control over is how we deal with these changes and more importantly how we manage and shape the changes that can occur within us.

It has been my observation that people's lives radically transform when they give themselves whole-heartedly to the process of personal change. Here are a few examples of the actual results that were achieved by clients that I have worked with over the years: Transformed and passionate relationship, massive increase in self-confidence, more quality time, finding a strong life purpose, significant increase in income, clearing of debts, a better and more system-driven business, feeling more energised, building a multi-million pound property portfolio, an amazingly abundant life, a healthy loss in weight, healthy gain in weight, transformation in personal management of money, living a more passionate and exciting life, greater sense of personal worth and more spiritual connection.

We don't have time to waste on the pages of this book. Your time is precious. The world moves faster now than ever before. Information comes to you at a rate that, quite frankly, is sometimes overwhelming, confusing and in many cases totally irrelevant. Therefore you will need to dig deep and find clarity in what you want to change and the new life (lifestyle) you want to live. At the same time, I will need to be clear with you, in what you need to do to get there. Hold onto your bootstraps, this is going to be an exciting and soul-searching journey.

In this chapter I want to share with you four ingredients that enable you to gracefully, intelligently, powerfully and objectively make positive change in your life.

It's Time To Commit

The first ingredient is commitment and that means putting action behind your words. So now we are starting our journey together and for it to be the most productive for you, I would like to make the following requests:

* ✦ *Get yourself a blank journal. It needs to be lined or plain and one that you feel comfortable capturing the lessons and change that you will experience.*

* ✦ *What I would like to ask is your permission to be 100% open and frank with you; to share an authentic and real message. In a nut shell, I would like your permission to be brutally honest with you throughout this book.*

So now we have reached a point where I would like to ask for your commitment; I have found that by putting your name against a commitment and doing so in writing massively increases your chances of succeeding. For that reason I would like to ask you to read and sign the following agreement:

Coaching, Mentoring & Commitment Agreement

I _____ (print your name here) give Dr Rohan Weerasinghe permission to be totally open and direct with me through the pages of this book. I am open to doing what I need to do in order to allow positive and life-shifting changes occur in my life. I understand that I will need to commit time and effort to this process and that nothing great is achieved without effort. I also accept that there are areas of my life that I have total control over and others areas that are outside of my control. I will not place blame on anyone else and fully accept that my responsibility is to take control of my thoughts and how I adapt to the world around me. I will not focus on those things that are out of my control. I will take on board all that I read that is applicable to my circumstances and I will commit for at least 90 days in order to create massive momentum. I have the power within me to do this, the courage to face the tough challenges, the passion to pursue my purpose and the love and spiritual abundance to help not just myself but others around me. This is my journey and I choose to take it. I am ready to be stretched physically and emotionally. I am ready to move on from where I am now with passion and enthusiasm. Nothing is going to stop me – bring it on.

Signed: _____ *Date:* _____

Awareness

It is my unequivocal believe that the fundamental basis for all change in our lives starts with 'Awareness' and this is Ingredient No. 2. I say to every one of my clients that awareness is the first step to change. I want you to become an Awareness Activator. In the same way that organisations like Alcoholics Anonymous work on the principle that a person must first acknowledge that he or she is an alcoholic, you and I must first develop an acute awareness of our pain, our circumstances and the things that we wish to change. It is even more subtle than that. Once you have started along the path of change, then you will experience what I call the 'Scale of Awareness'. The more change you experience, the further up the Scale of Awareness you will travel.

Awareness Level	Description
1	Acknowledgement that you have a problem or issue in your life.
2	Clarity on what the issue is and how it is impacting yours and others lives.
3	Identifying your own personal basic driving force needs, your core beliefs, values and the rules by which you have to satisfy them.
4	Identifying the personal basic driving force needs of your parents, partner and anyone that has a major influence on your life and the situation you are in right now. This may include understanding their core beliefs, values and the rules by which they live. At this level you are able to identify the root cause of your current challenge(s).
5	At this level of awareness you are able to acknowledge and observe the direct impact of your thoughts, beliefs, values and rules working in harmony with the universal laws of spirit and attraction. Through this awareness you are able to redefine how you see and experience the world.

As you work through this book I recommend that you check back in on this table to establish where your level of awareness is in different areas of your life. If, for example, you are feeling frustrated in a particular area of your life right now then simply acknowledge that this is the case. Frustration is usually a symptom of a problematic part of your life and by identifying this you are at Level 1 of awareness and this is the first step to change.

Let me give you an example to help you understand what I'm talking about.

The Angry Man
Michael's Journey Of Awareness

When I met my client Michael he approached me because he felt that "everything in his world including his business was falling apart and all these things were a result of other people". These were his words. When he first came to me, he told me that his father had died 11 years ago and that since that time his business, personal life, health and relationship had deteriorated.

Michael's greatest anger was with his father because when he passed away, the family discovered that he had accumulated over £150,000 in debt on gambling and online horse betting. The result was that Michael and his family had spent several years fighting off the debt collectors.

So when I met Michael he was in a 'dark place'. Michael was carrying a deep-rooted anger towards his father, which was spilling over into everything he did. He was acting with extreme caution in every deal and with every new client or associate. He trusted nobody. This lack of trust, anger and long-standing resentment towards his father was eating away at Michael's insides and prevented him from trying new projects or looking at opportunities.

The reality was that he had no awareness that the anger and resentment he held towards his father was the root cause of all the problems he was experiencing 11 years later. By taking him through an initial coaching process I was able to help Michael identify clearly that his problem was essentially down to where he had been putting his focus for the past 11 years. Once he saw this, it was like a light bulb had gone on for him and I asked him to acknowledge it clearly and boldly. For him this was Level 1 and 2 on the Scale of Awareness and with coaching he rapidly moved up to Level 5 awareness. In simple terms I helped him shift his focus so that Michael became one hundred percent aware that the problem was with him and not anybody or anything else.

Now he had taken back control we were able to start the Six Step Change Process.

There is an important message that I can share from Michael's story – you have control of all of your emotions. Every emotion that you are experiencing now can be understood and changed if you have the courage to take responsibility for that change. That does not mean it will be easy, nor does it mean that you only have to do it once and everything will be fine. The reality is that your life has to become a journey of exploration and growth. Yes you can make massive and inspiring life changes, however, it is what you then do on a consistent basis that will define the quality of your everyday life.

Become a Silent Witness

Years ago I heard the great author and speaker Dr Deepak Chopra use the term 'silent witness' in reference to the process of observing your spiritual being and your life experiences. I would highly recommend his book Synchro Destiny as it will help you understand how our thoughts and emotions can impact your body at a cellular level. On a personal level I found the term 'silent witness' extremely powerful, which is why I'm including it as the third ingredient to making effective changes in your life. I use this philosophy in virtually every area of my life and have since explored and expanded the concept into a much broader context when working with audiences and clients on a one-on-one basis. I would like to therefore invite you to be a silent witness throughout this book and during your journey of change and beyond.

What I mean by silent witness in the context of this book is to become an objective, non-judgemental observer of yourself and your immediate world around you in order to better understand how and why you do what you do. The best approach to this is to mentally step outside or float outside of your body and then consciously imagine you are standing, or sitting down observing yourself in that moment. This is an important distinction. You have to be able to objectively look, see, hear and feel what might be happening, at that unique moment in time. I want you to imagine that you did not know this person that you are watching (you) and ask some of the following searching questions. Note that where I make reference to 'this person', I am referring to you:

Silent Witness:

Observational Questions

> What is the root cause of this person's pain?
>
> What caused this person to react like that?
>
> If they continue to think and act this way where could it ultimately end up?
>
> How much pain is this person's behaviour causing other people?
>
> How much of the situation is outside of this person's control?

Silent Witness:

Solution Questions

> What can this person change in their language pattern to improve their situation?
>
> What beliefs would they need to adopt to radically change their life & situation?
>
> What things could this person be grateful for in their life right now?
>
> What three suggestions to help them move forward would you tell them right now?

Hopefully you are getting a strong sense of the penetrative power of this process. As you become familiar with the process of being a silent witness, you will tune into tiny little things that you and others do and say. You will be able to shift your focus back and forth from being the person in the experience to the person watching the experience. That gives you a real edge and allows you to choose to be objective in troubled times.

You are now officially a silent witness – thoughtful, insightful, respectful, non-judgemental and wise. It's a pleasure to meet you.

It's Time For Acceptance

The fourth ingredient for effective change is Acceptance. The situation you are in is exactly what it is, and it has occurred at this time in your life for a specific reason. As part of this process of change that you are now going through, it is vital that you completely understand and accept that your life will follow cycles; some of which will be directly influenced by you and others that will happen around or to you. For many people this can be a hard pill to swallow. For example, I often meet people who will describe their situation and although it is clear from the conversation that they are the primary cause of their problem, they will continually look for an external reason (blame) for why this part of their life is upside down.

On the other hand, I also meet people who have such a need to be in control of their whole world that they refuse to acknowledge that there are some things outside of their immediate control. As a result they will often say "you don't understand, my life seems to be out of control and it is because all these bad things keep happening to me."

If you find yourself feeling the same way as the people I have described above, then remember that if you spend your time blaming external circumstances and/or focusing on not being able to control your circumstances – then subconsciously you are giving the responsibility of your current situation to a force outside your control. You are releasing responsibility for your life.

Environmental cycles

Environmental cycles are events that happen around us that have a direct or indirect impact on our lives. It can be anything from a very immediate issue with a loved one to an economic issue on a global level. Whether it is a small or large event, we experience these external influences in cycles and they are continually happening in the outside world. It is generally only when these events come into contact with our lives in a direct way that we can be influenced. It is how you adapt to this change around you that will define where you end up next.

Working from the premise that it is not what happens to you that ultimately defines your path but rather how you react, adapt and change to these external circumstances, then the true power of your ability to change lies in the control you have over your inner world and what I call your Emotional Cycles.

Emotional Cycles

These are internal cycles that occur as a direct result of the feelings that you experience on a consistent basis. They impact directly on how you show up in the world on a day-to-day basis. These emotional cycles affect the way you think, the way you feel, the way you communicate, the way you operate in your work and social environment. In simple terms, emotional cycles massively control the quality of your life from the inside-out. If you can control these cycles, then in any situation you can control the way you feel. Typical emotions that you can choose to feel include:

Disempowering	Empowering
Hopelessness	Hope
Depression	Courage
Fear	Expectation
Sadness	Happiness
Lost	Directed
Untrustworthy	Trusting
Apathy	Excitement
Laziness	Motivated
Impotence	Aroused
Drained	Energised
Unhealthy	Healthy
Indifference	Focused
Frustration	Motivated
Anger	Forgiveness
Directionless	Purposeful
Unloved	Loving
Unworthy	Empowered
Empty	Spiritual

Even without anything happening in your external world, you have the ability to place a thought in your mind, which then creates any of the above emotional responses. Think about it for just a minute. I can almost guarantee that there has been a time in the past when somebody has let you down; in particular somebody that you were very close to and whom you trusted. I am also sure that you have the ability to reflect on that occasion right now and in an instant you will probably have one of two emotions, but you will not be able to experience both at the same time. You will either have the feeling of anger towards that person, which you have not let go of, or you will have a calm sense of forgiveness towards that person. Only you know which of those two emotions you feel towards that person right now.

Remember, you are the one that controls which of those two emotions you feel at any one moment. Don't get me wrong, that does not mean it will always be easy to shift your focus and control your emotional response. That comes with time, practice, a deep sense of a greater universe and a heart that can love unconditionally irrespective of what happens to you or how much hurt you may feel. The exciting thing to grab hold of here is the very fact that you can choose how you want to feel in any situation. In some cases you may not choose to control your emotions, you may wish to let them just flow. But should you need to be resourceful, to gain clarity and take control quickly of a situation, you now have the awareness than you control the flow and impact of your emotions – instantly.

2 | Seven Blocks That Crush Positive Change

Introduction

Have you ever noticed how we each have a completely different perception of the world? I personally believe that when people fail at something they are trying to succeed at, their belief of why they have apparently failed can only be based on their own personal perception. They have created a reality in their minds based on their life up until that point.

For the remaining part of this book I would like to request that you put aside any 'baggage' or past perceptions of the subjects that we discuss. Allow yourself the opportunity to explore the subjects and if you feel a resistance, be a silent witness in that moment and ask why you think this may be coming up.

During this chapter I will be describing certain characteristics of people who do not succeed in their endeavours, who are unable to make positive changes in their lives or who reach blocks in their life and cannot move beyond them. My intention here is not to focus on the negative or be critical, but rather to make you aware of these characteristics and patterns in the hope that as a silent witness you may spot something that you can change quickly. The fact is that when you set off to achieve a dream or overcome a challenge in any area of your life, your goal is not to fail; your goal is to succeed. If you do not achieve this goal, then it is important to identify the reasons why and raise your awareness, so that you can avoid making the same mistakes in the future.

The Blocks To Positive Change

Why have I named them 'The seven blocks to positive change?' Firstly let me repeat my premise that if you decide that you passionately want to change a specific area of your life then your primary focus is to be able to fulfil this dream. You certainly don't set out with a view to failing. The habits that typically lead to non-achievement of any goal must be seen as blocks or obstacles. Actually there are many such destructive habits, but there are certain blocks that are much more common than others. Over years of working with people from across the globe, I have boiled these down to the Seven Blocks To Positive Change.

Whenever I am coaching or mentoring somebody one of the first things I help them to do is identify their limiting beliefs or bad habits. As soon as those limiting beliefs have been identified, the client is able to take complete ownership of each bad habit or limiting belief. It then becomes a conscious choice to allow it to happen or not. This is incredibly empowering. Without that awareness, the same limiting beliefs and habits can continually repeat themselves for days, months and years without ever being noticed.

Creating awareness is the first step to taking back control of your life

Block No. 1: Repeating The Same Habits

You may be familiar with the phrase that is often quoted form Albert Einstein "The definition of insanity is doing the same thing and expecting a different result."

As simple as this phrase may appear, it is actually very profound because as human beings we do have a tendency to repeat things again and again in our lives with a subconscious hope that we will be able to create a different outcome. The following two examples illustrate how this shows up on a practical level.

Example 1

A couple in a relationship have reached a block and constantly seem to find themselves arguing. The arguments are usually triggered by one or two minor issues that would have been totally ignored when they first met. However, now, whenever the trigger occurs they follow the same argument pattern. The issue does not get resolved, they both get frustrated and it usually ends with one of them walking away from the argument. Things cool off and then one week later, the trigger occurs again, and the pattern becomes repeated. Both of them want to break the pattern but continue the same arguments in hope that one of them will concede and then 'it will all work out'. It rarely does and the relationship heads down a slippery slope.

Example 2

You open up your bank statement at the end of the month only to discover that your bank account is overdrawn. You cannot understand how your account could be in a negative position. You look over the entries in your bank statement to see if there is anything obvious that has caused your account to go into overdraft. However, there just seems to be a series of small purchases, nothing major. You resolve to be more careful over the next month with your spending. However, each of the following months produces similar results with an account that gradually gets more and more negative. You continue the same process, not changing anything dramatic in the hope that you will miraculously start spending significantly less to allow the account to come back towards zero. You are unclear, slightly fearful of how to resolve it and keep doing the same thing. It slowly starts to feel like there is no way out.

You may not even be aware that you are actually repeating habits, thought processes, conversations or even internal conversations on a consistent basis. More often than not we aren't aware because we only see the world through our own eyes. This is why it's so important to take the time to raise your awareness and become a silent witness to your own habits. This is not about judgement – this about understanding. Let us briefly explore the dangers of repeating old habits that are not serving us.

Old Habits Die Hard – So They Say

I do not know your personal circumstances. However I do know that by picking up this book there must be something in your life right now that you have a deep desire to change. Having reached this point, it is highly likely that the internal process and habits that you have adopted are not helping you to break out of your current cycle of thinking or feeling. The issue is not with the outside world, it is with your inner world.

These habits occur on a daily, hourly or even minute-by-minute basis. To simplify it, there are essentially three forms of habit you should look out for:

1. *Emotional*

2. *Physical*

3. *Intellectual*

These three forms of habit tend to repeat themselves again and again and as they continue over many years they form cycles that we are not even aware of. Some can serve us in a positive way whilst others can be highly destructive.

Emotional cycles involve us allowing specific emotions to come to the surface very quickly in response to a set of external circumstances. For example, somebody who has a lot of pain associated with their current financial situation will often feel tense and stressed even at the thought of a bank statement coming through the post. At the mention of finance, borrowing money or having to read a bank statement, they will completely switch off. They may even close down in order not to have to face their financial circumstances. Their subconscious goes into a protective mode.

Physical cycles are essentially habits that we do with our bodies. This can be something as simple as eating habits like continuing to feed our bodies bad quality food when we are feeling emotionally insecure. Another example might be the habit of drinking too much on a regular basis or even smoking and taking drugs. It can also include apathy, weak body language, the way we carry our body and even lack of exercise. Body language habits play a massive role in how we feel and act. Often we stand, sit, move and breathe in specific ways in reaction to certain circumstances. Without realising it, these physiological responses can magnify our emotional response. Your face is often the very first place that this shows up, even on the most minute level – a twinge or a wince.

Intellectual cycles are the logical element to the whole process. This is where a situation arises and we intellectually apply logic to why we should or should not take a specific action. For example, I meet people who want to leave their current job situation. They are frustrated, feel undervalued and underpaid and want to do something different like starting a business. However, they use the recession or their husband, wife or family as their logical reason why it would not be a good time to start a business now. Another term you may have heard is paralysis of analysis. Risk aversion falls under this category. I cannot count the number of people that I have met who never even started on the path to financial freedom because they thought too much about what problems and risks might happen. Imagine what their lives could be like now.

It is absolutely correct that if a person is not aware of these habits and does not have the tools to change, then old habits do die hard. As you read and work through this book you have the opportunity to remove any destructive habits and create new empowering ones.

Stop The Cycle In Its Tracks

If a cycle of behaviour is not helping you in any way then you must to stop it now. If it is not giving you a sense of worth and making you feel better about who you are, then you must stop it now. If this cycle has continued for some time and you have not positively changed or moved forward in that specific area of your life then you must stop it now. If you don't, then in reality the rest of this book is of no value to you whatsoever. That is the cold hard truth.

I would like to give you two rapid tools for stopping these self-destructive cycles.

Refocus – whenever you focus on something with enough intensity, the thing that you are focusing on becomes magnified. As simple as this may sound it is true for anything that you do. For example when something good happens in your life and you focus and celebrate it, you find yourself feeling better and often other good things around you tend to get magnified and feel great. If you are frustrated in your working environment and your job is getting you down, the more you focus on the feelings that you are experiencing, the more depressed you will become. In the instant that you find yourself entering one or more of the negative habits (emotional, physical or intellectual) described, you must immediately change your point of focus to something much more empowering.

We can actually do this together right now. Just for a moment, I want you to think about one of the areas in your life that is distressing you or causing you discomfort. Notice how you feel about it, how it makes your body feel, your stomach and what images appear in your mind. Hold that thought in your mind and allow the feelings to come over you.

Now, if you are sitting down, please stand up. If you can, gently jump up and down on the spot and if you can't, move some part of your body to get the blood flowing. As you do this I want you to think about one thing that has made you laugh in the past – anything. You can also think about one thing that you are really grateful for in your life. It could be the smile from a friend; it could be your parents, children, a lover, a business opportunity, your health, the feeling of the sun when it spreads warmth on your face. ANYTHING.

Now hold out your arms and close your eyes, keep thinking about the funny moment in your life or the thing that you are grateful for. Breathe deep and say 'thank you' out loud. Repeat it several times. As you do this smile and I mean really smile. If you have a mirror nearby look in the mirror and look yourself in the eye and just grin with lots of teeth. Say 'thank you' again. Notice how you feel. Do you feel silly, happy, stupid, grateful, funny or a mixture of all? Now stop. Allow your breathing to calm, close your eyes and notice the blood flowing through your veins and the feeling of energy around your body.

There are two things I would like you to observe about what we have just done. Firstly, I took you on a journey asking you to move your body, then to visualise something and to engage your whole body in a complete shift of focus. I have no doubt that if you did the full exercise you will be feeling more invigorated and grateful now. And the heavy feeling you had before will have disappeared. You can do exactly the same thing for yourself at any moment in time. The key is to focus with intensity and clarity on something different and positive. If ever you attend one of my seminars, watch to see me use this with people that I work with in front of the audience. As simple as this may sound it works.

My message is simple here. Change your focus. You can break any emotional, physical or intellectual cycle by focusing on something different. You need to do it consistently, regularly and make the focus on something that is outside of your circumstances. The real goal is to make the focus toward something that has a positive outcome.

I want to point out here that I'm not suggesting that you ignore how you are feeling or what is going on in your life. The purpose here is to change your focus and break the repeated negative cycle or habit. Once you have done, you will move into a more resourceful state. We will cover this later in the book.

Move Your Body –   Let's expand on body movement. I would like to try something. Please stand up (assuming you are physically able to do so) and bounce up and down on your toes for approximately 60 seconds. If not, then wiggle your buttocks – do something. Once you have done that, make a mental note of how you feel. How is your energy? Can you feel a slight buzz in your body? How is your breathing? Just this simple act of standing up and bouncing can radically change your physical, emotional and intellectual state. Actually, the lymphatic system removes toxins from our body by a pumping action stimulated by simple up-and-down movement such as dancing or jogging. So from a purely logical perspective bobbing up and down can help you change the emotional state and cleanse your body.

I'm sure you've had the experience of listening to music and then dancing and feeling your mood change. Dance is a classic example of how you can use a change in physical state to break negative emotional cycles. Running or jogging has a similar impact. Breathing rapidly also changes your physical and emotional state. Smiling and singing does the same thing. Research has shown that this type of movement helps stimulate the production of serotonin, a chemical neurotransmitter in the brain that influences a variety of psychological and bodily functions. Serotonin influences brain cells that are related to our sex drive, our moods and even our appetite. It is also suggested by some researchers that lack of serotonin is one of the contributors for depression. Basically, if you are able to create more serotonin, you will generally feel better. Pretty cool when you think that you can create this chemical yourself by simply moving your body more.

The real impact of this is easy to measure for yourself. Simply try something radically different with your body. Stand up and walk around the room quickly. Dance. Put some music on. Scream and shout. Do something crazy or out of character. Have a drink of cold water. Go outside and breathe fresh air. Go and talk to somebody that you have never spoken to before. When you do this, make a mental note of how you feel and how quickly that change took place. It takes seconds for the effect to kick in.

When you combine a change in your physical state with a shift in your focus the impact becomes incredibly effective.

Block No. 2: Lack Of Purpose

I have dedicated a whole chapter to this subject and therefore I only want to briefly describe my view on this. I personally believe that this is singularly one of the most important reasons why people do not achieve their true potential. In times of challenge, when you are feeling desperate, or frustrated, or when you have a fear of moving forward, lack of purpose is the root that will anchor you to the ground and literally cripple you.

I believe that you can tell by watching someone and how they conduct themselves if they are living on purpose or not. The way a person carries himself or herself throughout the day, expresses emotions and moves from one activity to another is a direct reflection of the level of purpose that they are living. When a person is living on a day-to-day basis without any specific purpose they generally do the bare minimum to survive and typically live a lacklustre existence.

Lynne Twist, who wrote the book, The Soul of Money, is an amazing human being. Her purpose has taken her on a life journey of over 40 years of fundraising and working in leading positions in major global initiatives to end world hunger; to protect the rainforests; to improve health, economic, and political conditions for women; and to advance the scientific understanding of human consciousness. Just take a moment to read this last sentence again. Without knowing any more about Lynne Twist you can immediately have a sense that this is a person who wakes up every morning and lives her life with a massive sense of purpose. Actually, Lynn Twist has helped raise hundreds of millions of dollars towards global causes and continues to change the lives of millions of people with her teaching and compassion.

When somebody has this level of purpose in their life then failure is not an option. When something does not work, or they experience loss or grief, these people see it as a chance to learn, grow and become stronger on their path to achieving their greater vision.

My Mum's Story

I have personally experienced the loss of a close family member in my life. Through this grief I have witnessed how a bigger purpose can create inspiring changes in the people who have experienced the loss. When my father died, I was only 13 years of age and my brothers Marcus and Jason were 12 and 9-years-old respectively. My mother was in her early 30s and in her darkest hours she knew that now she had a greater purpose beyond the massive sense of loss that she was experiencing. For many years during my father's repeated strokes and minor heart attacks, my mother had loved and cared for both him and the three of us. Now having lost the man she loved, she knew that her life purpose was to bring her three sons up as best she could, to provide food, shelter, different life experiences and a loving home.

This became my mum's purpose in life for the next five to ten years and beyond. Through emotional and financial challenges, my mum woke each day with this one purpose in her heart. It was this inspiring shift that helped each of us to grow into the men that we are today.

Many people ask me when I am speaking, how can I find my purpose and many believe that making more money will help them do that.

Sadly this is a false illusion. For now, don't worry too much about this question. Just allow yourself to listen to the voice in your heart and your intuition about what excites and feels right for you. We'll talk later about this.

Block No. 3: **Procrastination**

The *Oxford English Dictionary* defines procrastination as "to delay doing something that you should do, usually because you do not want to do it". I personally think this is not completely accurate. Procrastination has many faces and in some cases yes, we put things off because we simply do not want to do them. On the other hand there are things that we do want to do, however something else that we also have the choice to do seems more important at that moment and so we choose to do the other activity first. The problem gets worse when we keep bringing up *other* activities that seem more important than the one that we know we should do.

Emotional procrastination

This form of procrastination tends to exists at a subconscious level. It is caused by a set of limiting beliefs that you have about life or the task that you have to do. It may be that you have a fear related to the activity, you do not believe you can achieve it, possibly a low self-esteem in this area, some sort of guilt associated with the activity or simply a feeling that the activity would make you feel uncomfortable. If these beliefs are strong enough and you can justify them to yourself on a consistent basis then the activity will never take place. You literally talk yourself out of doing it.

Remember that *awareness* is the first step to change. In order to overcome emotional procrastination you must:

1. *Start to list all the things you say to yourself about why you have not taken action. I mean everything you say – these are your reasons or excuses. My guess is that you*

should very quickly be able to see a pattern forming that will reveal some of your restrictive beliefs linked to procrastination.

2. *For every reason or excuse that you write down in Step 1, replace that statement with a positive affirmation AND link it directly with your higher purpose and vision. This gives you a stronger reason to get it done. The following story is a great example of this.*

3. *The last thing here is to write down the cost to you and your family if you don't take action on the things that you know you want to achieve. This is where you start to associate pain with procrastination. I am laying seeds here for a deeper discussion later in the book.*

Ian's Story

Very recently I was running a three-day seminar on the subject of personal growth and financial independence through property investing. On the second day a smart-looking gentlemen in his mid-late thirties walked up to me and said,

"Hi, my name is Ian and I am loving the weekend but feel I am too comfortable in my life right now. I earn over £60,000 per year and although I can see this is an excellent opportunity for me I don't have any great motivation to take action. In fact it has been like that now for about 8 years or more. I think I need a kick up the backside."

I said to him, *"Ian, actually, what you really need are three things (1) A purpose (2) A mentor to guide you and kick you up the bum (3) A complete realisation of the cost for not taking action."*

His procrastination to develop a property business came partly from being too comfortable, but the biggest thing was not having a deep driving reason to step out of his cosy lifestyle. He seemed like a warm person who was obviously smart enough and open to new ideas, so I asked a few more questions. Then I hit his hot button; he wanted to start a family and did not want to have to be a working father. He had watched his father work 12/14-hour days for years, always coming back late and exhausted every day. Through this high stress work pattern his father developed a serious illness and in his late forties became virtually housebound. Ian absolutely did not want that for his kids.

It was clear – at that moment in his life, Ian's driving passionate PURPOSE was to be able to watch his children grow up, and be there when he chose to be and not when his boss allowed him to be. I worked with him to really reinforce what it might cost him, I asked what it would feel like if his kids got to 10 years of age and had only seen him for an hour or two a day for those 10 years. At this point his face literally changed. He went almost pale and his facial muscles visibly dropped. At that moment, he was reliving his childhood and the experience he had had with his dad. Even I could feel his pain. In this emotional place, no amount of job income or comfort could stop him doing what was needed to break free.

This was his tipping point. He looked me in the eye, and said *"Thank you. Now I understand. I am not prepared to waste another 10 years making excuses and procrastinating. I really want to have a mentor to help me on this path, what do you suggest?"*

I then reminded him he should first go away and create a new mantra. A daily declaration that re-affirms that he is an action taker working towards being a full-time dad for his future kids.

Ian was open to change. By identifying the blockage (comfort), establishing the cost to him if he carried on with it, he was able to put a new action in place to break the blockage. With some one-on-one mentoring and coaching to give him direction he was on his way.

Environmental procrastination

Interestingly, environmental procrastination is a lot more common than people might think. A simple example of this is if you have a working area that is extremely cluttered with paperwork, books, magazines and lots of other things around you, then this can seriously affect your sense of clarity. You feel overwhelmed by your environment even before you start the task at hand. The result is usually a lack of motivation and inactivity. Sound familiar? I believe this is such a big issue in today's world that I have dedicated a whole chapter to this subject later in the book.

There are other environmental influences such as distractions, opportunities that come your way during the course of the day, other pieces of work that remain unfinished, noise, e-mails, phone calls and pretty much anything else that comes into your immediate environment on a daily basis. All these things have the potential to distract you from your daily purpose.

Some people set themselves up for procrastination by creating an environment that simply does not allow them to focus on the tasks at hand. In doing this they continually perpetuate the process of procrastinating and although they may appear busy, they are not really getting the essential activities completed. I have been guilty of this in the past. On occasions when there have been too many opportunities, too many 'things' that I wanted to do, I convinced myself that these were very important. The result was that I got bogged down and became frustrated that I could not achieve them all. An example of this for me was writing this first book. Although I had written many notes, and been planning to do it for several years, other things came up that stopped it getting written. It took a decision, a change of priorities and the commitment to take on a great book coach, Mindy Gibbins-Klein, that finally broke the inertia and it worked.

In Chapter 8 we will discuss very specific ways to change your environment in order to move forward and overcome procrastination and apathy.

Time-management procrastination

This type of procrastination occurs as a result of conscious decisions made on a daily basis. What I am referring to here relates to not understanding how to manage your time, not knowing how to prioritise activities, not being able to break down tasks and delegate, or simply not having sufficient information to complete certain activities. The result is procrastination.

Poor time management is the seed of daily procrastination. By first identifying that you are consciously not managing your time properly you can choose to develop better time management skills. There are some very powerful questions that you can ask yourself that will help you deal with activities and overcome time management procrastination:

> *What additional information do I need to help me move forward?*
>
> *Who do I know that has been in this situation and can help me?*
>
> *What skills and knowledge do I need to move beyond this current block?*
>
> *How can I be more efficient with my time when dealing with this task?*
>
> *What is the most important activity that I need to focus on first?*
>
> *Which part of this work can be delegated to somebody else?*

On a personal level, in my businesses, the last point was one of the most important items that changed the way I operated my life. By first engaging a Personal Assistant many years ago, rather than trying to do everything myself, I was able to create space to be more effective. As obvious as this is, I have met hundreds of people who do not do this.

Block No. 4: Fear

At some level we all have fears. Please understand this and don't let pride switch off your brain at this point. Tune in, be a silent witness and notice where you are most resistant and that will stem from some form of fear or sense of insecurity in that area. In this section I'm referring to the larger fears that surround you as an individual. These deeper-rooted fears typically have a knock-on effect on the smaller activities that need to be carried out on a day-to-day basis.

Fear is real to the person who experiences it and unless addressed it will sit and fester.

Think for a moment about having a personal vision to create a lifestyle of time freedom and abundance for you and your family in the next few years. This is a big vision and in order to achieve it there will be hundreds of tasks needed to complete your goal. Imagine now that there are certain fears and beliefs that you hold about the world based on your life experiences to date. If these fears are sufficiently strong enough, they will block you from achieving many of your goals. The chances are, you will procrastinate and eventually stop pursuing the original goal.

I have listed out below examples of real fears that have been expressed by some of my clients from all over the world. You may wish to put a cross next to any that you relate to:

- [ ] *fear of success*`
- [ ] *fear of the unknown*
- [ ] *fear of failure*
- [ ] *fear of being laughed at*
- [ ] *fear of getting something wrong*
- [ ] *fear of losing money*
- [ ] *fear of getting your hopes up and then not succeeding*
- [ ] *fear that you let your family down*
- [ ] *fear that you do not have the ability to succeed*
- [ ] *fear that you're not good enough*
- [ ] *fear that you're not worthy enough*

If I had to single out one fear above all else that stops people moving forward, the **fear of failure** is the most dominant fear.

Let's look at fear of failure in the context of some of the most successful people that we see today. No matter what profession you look at, be it sport, politics, business, TV and movies, anybody who has achieved any level of success has got there through experiencing several failures and set-backs. Let's take Tiger Woods as an example. In his career as a golfer he achieved his greatness by practicing relentlessly and playing tournament after tournament from a young age. Part of this process included missing a lot of shots, by losing tournaments, by striking the ball incorrectly sometimes and consistently picking up his golf club and trying again and again and again. In doing this he refined his game to a point of being arguably the best golfer in history. Yes he has a great talent, but the talent alone was not enough. Tiger Woods did not let the fear of failure or missing a shot stop him from moving forward – he simply used it to sharpen his senses.

Mark Victor Hansen apparently experienced bankruptcy before then going on to write multi-million bestselling books like *Chicken Soup For The Soul.* Colonel Sanders in his late 60s drove around the USA trying to sell his Kentucky fried chicken recipe and was rejected by over 1000 people before somebody actually said "yes" to taking his recipe and developing it. KFC is now one of the most successful franchises in the world. Abraham Lincoln failed in business over many years before becoming president of the United States. Robert Kiyosaki, author of the global best-selling book *Rich Dad Poor Dad* was at one time around $400,000 in debt and came back to become a multimillionaire and develop one of the most successful education companies in the world. Donald Trump, at one point, when his business was struggling had reported liabilities of the order of $900 million.

Many great actors and actresses have ended up in alcohol rehabilitation centres after experiencing fame and not being able to handle it. The truly great ones dealt with this fear and came back to touch our lives at a greater level. The actor Robert Downey Jr is a great example of this. His career suffered when he went through a period of substance abuse and several arrests. When things got really bad he finally sought help. He is reported to have said *"You can reach out for help in kind of a half-assed way, and you'll get it, and you won't take advantage of it. It's not that difficult to overcome these seemingly ghastly problems... what's hard is to decide to actually do it."* The result was not only recovery from substance abuse but a complete turning point in his acting career and to date he has received Golden Globe and Academy Award nominations for his performances. Anthony Robbins at the start of his career became around $700,000 in debt due to a bad business partner taking money from him and then went on to become the number one personal development speaker and coach in the world and multi-millionaire. Failure in life can occur and when it does, it is how you and I respond to it that ultimately defines our destiny and the character we develop.

> Fear and setbacks are part of the process of positive change and success. They come with the territory, so you are going to have to accept them rather than fear them. Get excited that out of change and setbacks comes greater growth way beyond the setbacks. What I also want to say to you here is that it is time to move on. If you don't, then your partner, your family, your future and ultimately your destiny could all be destroyed by this one thing. So have faith, trust the process and let's move on together.

Hopefully you are getting the picture here. The only way to deal with the fear of failure is to see it as a temporary setback and a learning experience that will help you improve and grow as a human being. The important thing to do is ask powerful questions each time you experience a setback. With each failure that you experience it gives you an opportunity to study and examine what went wrong and how you can do it better next time.

Block No. 5: Lack of Focus

Throughout this book you will observe certain themes that appear several times. *Focus* and *purpose* are intimately connected to everything you do. I'm sure you have had days where you feel extremely frustrated because although you had a goal for the day, lots of distractions came up which shifted your focus. At the end of that day you did not feel like you had not achieved what you set out to achieve at the start of the day. Let me share with you a simple but proven solution.

This is an important formula because if you can consistently work towards aligning your focus with your overall purpose, then you will find that you move so much faster in the direction that you want to go.

Unfortunately, and fortunately, we are able to shift our focus at the drop of a hat. This is a characteristic that we have from an early age. I remember when my daughter was around seven months old, I was amazed how she was able to be watching a Baby Einstein educational video, then at the same time she swung her head round to watch what I was doing at the computer and then she looked out the window for a minute at a rabbit playing in the field. During those few minutes she missed what was happening on the screen in front of her. But very quickly she became focused on the screen again – until the next distraction came along. Her attention span was very short due to all the distractions.

Exactly the same thing happens to us as adults, we allow small distractions to shift our focus. This stems from one of our basic human needs – to experience variety and stimulation. More often than not, the shift in focus results in us losing two or three hours of time on the project that we should have been focused on.

In his book *Tycoon*, Peter Jones talks about the power of focus and setting goals. In his early years as an entrepreneur he experienced one of his businesses failing. He learnt from this and created more focus in his next venture. In one example he refers to a goal he set himself in 1998 to achieve £12 million in sales by the end of the year. By achieving this goal he intended to reward himself with a Ferrari 550. By the April of 1999, his company had achieved sales of £13.9 million through refocusing himself and his employees on a consistent basis. As a result, he treated himself to the Ferrari. In order to ensure that both his company and his staff maintained focus, they monitor their performance on a daily and hourly basis. He states "some people may regard this as an exaggerated effort, but I think it is clearly one of the factors that have led to my business success. I learned that lesson from losing that first business, which has consequently proved valuable."

Two important lessons can be learnt from what Peter Jones shared. Firstly, the failure of his previous business, as we described previously, he took as a learning lesson about creating more focus and being more efficient in monitoring performance. Many would have taken that failure and used it as a reason not to try again. Secondly, to maintain focus you need to really check regularly on how well you are keeping to your original plan. Sustained focus is what we are talking about here – not occasional glimpses.

Create urgency

One powerful way to sharpen your focus is to create urgency around the tasks that you have in front of you. It is vital that you take control of your day rather than letting other people determine your timetable. All too often people allow large spaces of time to achieve their tasks or to make decisions and this creates a lack of urgency and allows space for other things to distract the main focus.

Years ago, Domino's Pizza, an American pizza franchise, made an announcement that changed the face of fast food delivery across the world and which ultimately catapulted Domino's into one of the largest pizza franchises in the USA. Customers were told that they would receive the pizza for free if it took longer than 30 minutes for the home delivery of the pizza. Just for a moment, think about the implications this has both on the company and the customer. The customers benefit massively because now they have the ability to receive their food in a specific time period. If the food arrives late they get a discount. The company benefits because the employees are much more focused on operating in an efficient manner to ensure that the pizzas are cooked and the delivery is sent on its way to arrive at the customer's door within 30 minutes. The overall result was that Domino's Pizza had a much more efficient workforce with a totally different level of motivation and the business grew to a whole other level.

Imagine an hourglass with the top part of the glass filled with sand and that each grain of sand was equivalent to a minute of your life and that the total amount of sand in the top was equal to your whole life from birth to death. Now imagine that as each grain pours through the neck into the lower part of the hourglass that minute upon minute of your life was passing by. As the upper part of the glass empties, what is left at the top is the amount of time you have left in your life. How much value would you put on every single minute that passes through the hourglass? The more time passes the greater you value your time. That is the level of urgency and value that you should place on your time every day.

> **Get focused. Get really focused. Stop allowing 'things' and your thoughts to distract you.** Two hours wasted doing something that is unproductive could be two hours spent walking through a forest with your family, loved one or children enjoying an amazing magical moment. Or those same two hours could be spent analysing a property deal or business opportunity that makes you £20,000 profit. Equally those same two hours could be spent exercising, meditating or preparing an amazing raw food meal to improve your physical and mental health. Get focused. Decide what is important and what is not important, then delegate the activities that are less important or that could be done by someone else so that you can be much more efficient with your time.

Block No. 6: Poor Diet and Fitness

What you eat and the level of your fitness can have a direct impact on your mood, attitude, health and general level of energy. If you want to be more effective at making life changes, feeling more vibrant on a daily basis and simply feeling better about yourself, then this is an area are of your life that makes a difference. I personally experienced a massive shift in my energy, health and clarity of mind when I changed what I ate and drank on a regular basis. Equally, having been somebody who throughout his life has been an active sportsman I have also experienced what happens when that level of activity drops as a result of working too hard and not taking the time to maintain fitness and health. I have witnessed people heal significant illnesses through a change in diet, I experienced energy levels shifting to a whole new level both in myself and those around me by simply changing the type of food that is eaten and the regularity and type of exercise I do.

You have probably at some point in your life said to yourself, "I want to get fitter, healthier and eat better." You would have said it for a reason and it is likely that that reason is because deep down you knew that it would help you feel better about yourself but also make you more resourceful on a day-to-day basis. This is not rocket science, you simply have to be committed and follow a simple formula. The results can be astounding and everyone I have worked with who has placed some effort in this area has reported a fantastic response in the way they feel and their effectiveness in the things they do.

The great thing is that you only have two areas that you will need to focus on. If you are already strong in these areas, I congratulate you and encourage you to see if you can take it to another level again. If not, then enjoy the journey!

1. **Physical Health** – I have used the term physical health rather than physical fitness to encompass both aerobic and muscular fitness. Many people join gyms and believe that getting fit means lifting weights on a regular basis and forget to also improve their cardiovascular health. From my own personal experience and observation, it is important to develop a balance between the two. The other extreme is people who go down to a gym, do 20 minutes on the treadmill without really raising the heart level and don't bother lifting any weights because they believe it is not important. They leave the gym believing that they have had a workout – sorry but if that is you, then you are deluding yourself. Actually, both your cardiovascular system and musculo-skeletal structure benefit from doing the two forms of exercise correctly, regularly and for certain durations. My suggestion is to seek out a great personal trainer to help you in this area.

2. **Dietary Health** – What I would like to do here is share with you my experience of what I have found that works for me and other people that I know who have adopted a similar lifestyle. When my mother developed cancer in 2002, I spent a lot of time researching the impact of diet on helping to beat major illnesses. Through a change in diet I not only noticed a difference in my own health and vitality, but also in her body's ability to fight back. Almost 10 years later, after only a minor operation back then and a much more balanced diet, my mum is turning 70 and loving life. The approach that I have found and have adopted ever since was to eat live foods and super-foods that add natural supplementation and that help alkalise, cleanse and energise the body naturally.

We will explore this exciting subject in Chapter 10 and so for now I would like you to be a silent witness and be aware of what exercise you are and aren't doing. Also, what foods you are putting in your body and monitor how you feel at certain times of the day. When does your energy go up and down? Notice the direct relationship between your energy, mental sharpness and what you eat.

Block No. 7 Lack of Persistence

Persistence is without doubt right up there as an essential characteristic for anyone wishing to break the chains of their existing circumstances and to move forward, or achieve success. There are different types of persistence. For example, someone who is working in a job for over 40 years could be regarded as persistent. This type of persistence, however, is generally born out of a need to pay the bills, look after the children and cover the mortgage; so although yes, they show persistence, most people in this situation do not have any other choice.

The challenge comes when you are in a situation where you do have a *choice* to quit what you have started and slip back into old habits, back into your physical or emotional comfort zone. When your livelihood does not depend on it, there is always the option to quit.

In the book *Think & Grow Rich*, Napoleon Hill dedicated a whole chapter to the subject of persistence. His studies revealed that this was one of the essential characteristics of the most successful and wealthiest men and women alive. One sentence that really stood out to me when I first read this book was:

"As one makes an impartial study of the profits, philosophers, miracle men, and religious leaders of the past, one is drawn to the inevitable conclusion that persistence, concentration and effort, and definiteness of purpose, were the major sources of their achievements."

Think about a few great movies that you have watched over the years. The most inspiring ones for me, especially those based on a true story, are the stories where our heroes go through the most gruelling emotional and physical challenges and then emerged as the victors. I find that watching a movie like this leaves me emotionally inspired. My message to you is that you have the lead role in your own movie. All you need to do is accept that problems will occur and challenges will come up and setbacks will happen and just like in the movies you need to find a way to persist and emerge as the victor. Have an optimistic, abundant outlook and focus on what you desire, not on the possibility of what could go wrong. This simple axiom will act as a pillar of strength in even the most challenging moments.

Nelson Mandela, Mother Teresa, Gandhi, Martin Luther King, Abraham Lincoln Franklin Roosevelt and Thomas Edison are just a few names that have become household, simply because they chose not to give up in the pursuit of their dream.

> *What do you stand for?*
>
> *What is your purpose?*
>
> *What do you believe in strongly enough that you will keep going against all odds?*

Remember this – if you are not persistent in the pursuit of your dream then ultimately you will be persistent in the pursuit of somebody else's dream. As you read through this book, I believe that you will develop the tools and the vision to be persistent in overcoming challenges and moving towards your true passion and purpose.

In the words of Peter Jones, *"Stay determined. Never give up unless circumstances dictate and you need to regroup... Keep moving forward, always."*

My Message to Couples

Many of the issues we have discussed in this section can rear their heads in a relationship to such an extent that they create resentment, anger and frustration. Naturally this chapter is an opportunity to grow as an individual and if you don't have a significant other (partner) then I would recommend you do this with someone you have a deep trusting relationship with. If you are in a relationship, it is also an opportunity for you to grow with your partner by sharing openly and without judgement.

Therefore I would recommend that you approach this in the following way:

1. Work through the seven blocks separately and write out how you think each of these blocks may have shown up in your own personal life.

2. Next take an evening together and share with your partner what you have written down in your journal. Share first and then give each other the opportunity to comment without judgement – simply make observations that can help each other. Discuss positive ways to improve and avoid the old patterns in the future.

3. Finally, explore how you as a couple have operated together and where the blocks have shown up in some of the things that you have been doing. Ask questions in an open and frank way and look to find solutions rather than reasons. Ask yourself how we can work together to improve in the future and avoid getting caught by these blocks in the future.

3 | Give Yourself A Massive Prod

Introduction

I would like to use the word *PROD* as an acronym for helping you to make the necessary changes in your life right now. There are several dictionary definitions for the word prod including nudge, poke, kick and to rouse or urge to action. In reality, each of us does need a massive prod at some point in our lives when we have reached a standstill or cannot get off the starting blocks. Coaching is a form of prodding that creates focused results. You must learn to coach yourself at times and to allow yourself to be coached. The acronym 'prod' in this context will help you make the next big step towards the Six Step Change Process and beyond. So let's look at what PROD is.

Perception – In order to experience positive changes in your life, you may have to change your perception about your current situation and the world around you. In other words, change the meaning of what you see, hear and feel about your circumstances.

Responsibility – What I am going to ask you to do here is to take full responsibility for your circumstances and the way you are feeling. I realize something extremely tragic may have happened in your life, and it is difficult to grapple with how you might take responsibility for that. In a situation like this, I am referring more to taking responsibility for how you react now by changing your perspective.

Ownership – What I would like to say here is simple. You own your life. You own your emotions. You own every cell in your body and all the amazing gifts that are within you. Whilst you are on this earth in a conscious state, you have ownership over your physical and emotional being. Knowing that you have full ownership makes it much easier to take responsibility for how you react and operate in the world.

Decisive – Indecisiveness is one of the major causes of continuous failure. The opposite of this is being decisive. In order to be more decisive, you will have to take on board the skills used in asking questions and then getting a clear perspective, taking ownership and responsibility for what you are prepared to do and what will happen as a result. Not all decisions will lead to the result you are expecting. That is ok too and you will learn from that.

So let's take a look of each of these in more detail and as we do, I would like you to quietly ask yourself where in your life right now, can you apply this.

Perception (PROD)

There is no better place to start giving yourself a prod than with a change in perception. As you will discover later in this book, your perception is based essentially on the beliefs that you have developed throughout your life. There is a part of the brain called the Reticular Formation, located in the core of the brain stem and it is one of the oldest formations of the brain. It serves several roles, one of which is to help the brain filter certain information. In this way, the brain learns to ignore stimuli that are not considered important and at the same time it can help the brain become more sensitive to other things. Let me share an example of how this can dramatically impact relationships between two people.

Sarah and Michael's Story

Sarah is a client I worked with some years ago. She was in her late 40s, a smart woman and a very successful senior manager for a retail company. At the time that I met her she was on the verge of leaving her husband, Michael. She was fed up with the fact that their relationship had lost its spark and that he did not pay any attention to her anymore (to paraphrase her words). The issue that arose in the coaching was how she should go about telling him she wanted to leave him. She felt that it was out of her hands because he just was not doing anything to make the relationship work.

My role as her coach was to serve her and give her a chance to look at the situation from a different perspective. So I simply asked Sarah that if she were Michael, what would his description of the relationship be and how would he describe her role in the relationship. Immediately when I asked this question her whole body language and attitude changed. At no point up until then had she really even considered this – she had been so angry and frustrated.

I took Sarah through a variety of different experiences and their daily interactions from Michael's perspective. I asked her to be a Silent Witness and to shift her perception as though looking through his eyes and heart. This change in perspective suddenly enabled her to see where she had also become lazy in the relationship. She noticed things about the way she spoke to him, like the tone in her voice. She also noticed how little affection or contact she showed towards Michael because of her frustration in their relationship.

I then asked her to describe how she was when they first met. I asked her to imagine how Michael would have described her when they first met. Again this shift in perception back to their early years was a big revelation for her. Her perception shifted another 180°.

From this process alone, she was able to see that actually she could take responsibility for her part in how this relationship could grow rather than lay blame. She had no illusion that it would take work and a much greater level of intimate communication with Michael and that she was prepared to do that rather than let the marriage end in divorce.

If I were illustrating this with you face-to-face, I would give you a pair of sunglasses with blue coloured lenses and ask you to tell me what colour the things around you appear to be. At the same time I would be wearing a pair of red tinted glasses. It is highly likely that you would tell me that most of the things that you can see have a blue tint to them. I on the other hand, would be telling you that all I can see is red. The point being that we are both looking at the same thing but our perception is based on the filter through which we are looking.

This is the very reason two people can argue for hours over one subject, because each has developed a perception around their belief of the subject. Both are convinced they are right and refuse to switch glasses for moment. Sound familiar?

What many people are not aware of is that this filtering system is sensitive to our emotional state. In other words, the more distressed or emotionally charged we are about a situation, the stronger the filter becomes. Put another way, when you are experiencing pain, frustration, adversity or loss, your conscious mind becomes even more focused on the very thing that you are experiencing most. If, for example, you are feeling broke or in financial distress, then you will find yourself seeing and experiencing more bills, bank charges or demand letters. You will literally have the perception that you are drowning in your own debt. If your business is not working out or struggling, you will notice more problems with the economy or changes in the market to justify why this is happening to you. The same thing happens in every area of your life.

If you don't take off the sunglasses and put on a different pair with a completely different shade of colour nothing will change for you. The sunglasses represent your perception of the world and with the role that the reticular formation plays in the brain.

What I'm saying here is that your reality is based wholly on your perception of what your reality really is. In other words, it's as real as you choose to make it.

So if you are able to change your beliefs and your perception the result will be a completely different reality. We will tackle beliefs in a subsequent chapter. There is, however, one vital stage to the process of changing your perception and that is to see your situation as it is. Not worse or better, just as it is.

See It As It Is First

When I talk about changing your perspective I am not suggesting here that you ignore your current circumstances and simply look at the world through rose tinted glasses. The reality of the situation is that something is not right in your life. It may even be that you have genuinely experienced something extremely painful or hurtful. Maybe your partner has left you or cheated on you. It could be that you are facing bankruptcy or you have lost your job. Your business may be at the brink of collapse. Or, it may be that someone dear to you has passed away and you are feeling a massive sadness and sense of loss. If you are experiencing something like this right now, then it is extremely real to you.

Many people fall into the trap of seeing or imagining these things a lot worse than they actually are. This is self-destructive. What you must do in any situation you face is see your circumstances as they are now and not how they might be. Don't allow yourself to see things any worse than they are. Don't imagine how bad it could get in the future and don't exaggerate the situation. Simply be clear on what your actual circumstances are.

Capture the physical nature of the situation and how you feel in your journal. The experience of doing this often leads to a sense of relief. In seeing the current situation as it is and not any worse, there is a subconscious process that takes place in your mind of letting go. You have now identified the real picture. You've recorded it on paper and you can take a deep breath and say, 'okay, so this is where I am right now'. It is what it is – now you can focus on the solution and the changes you wish to make.

A Personal Share – My Divorce

When I was 34 years of age I went through a separation into a divorce and for a period moved back to my mother's home. Initially this was a shock to me. Here I was, someone who is regarded as being successful in their career, living in a small room that I originally stayed in when I was 18 years of age. I can still remember the series of negative questions I asked myself relating to my success as a person and in my marriage. When this happened, for a short period I remember looking out into the future and having several negative thoughts, which were all based on my beliefs and previous perceptions about divorce. I started to see my situation a lot worse. I had feelings of guilt and self-blame. I had always strived for success and here I was failing in a marriage. It felt deeply painful. It is easy in these situations to allow self-pity and self-doubt to set in. It seems a long time ago now and it is hard to believe that I was that person – but the reality was that in that unique situation and point in my life this was my perception of the world.

Thankfully, through reading, personal growth, coaching, friends and good family support I consciously changed my perception. I took a good look at my situation and saw it as it was. I took full responsibility for what had happened. I also reminded myself that the only person who is in control of my life is me. At that stage there, I started to make clear, forward-thinking decisions. I took time to write down what I really wanted in my life. I also put the intention into the universe that I wanted to give more of myself and to help others. I also used this experience as a chance to understand how

I could be better in my next relationship. These actions combined, helped me get clarity and develop a greater sense of purpose.

Within months I found myself in Turkey after two earthquakes had taken tens of thousands of lives. I spent my millennium new year there with my younger brother Jason helping build shelters, schools and helping families relocate. At this point I had a greater calling and higher sense of purpose. My perception was rapidly changing and over the next few years I travelled, worked abroad and met an amazing lady and today we have a lovely daughter.

How To Change Your Perception

There is not one simple solution to changing your perception. Some people might say "Oh, just snap out of it and look on the bright side". For some people that may work. If that is not you, then I have three Perception Altering Approaches. Actually, each of these is a role that you can play. Remember, you are re-writing each chapter in a book called My Life, so you get to choose which character or role you would like to play.

The Silent Witness – Here we are again with our old friend the silent witness. We are going to use this slightly differently now. I'd like you to close your eyes and take three slow deep breaths and imagine your current situation, the one that is giving you the most trouble at present. Put yourself in the position of experiencing it right now. If there are other people involved put them in the scene too. Once you have a specific scene in your mind, mentally float out of your body and sit or stand next to yourself and start to make objective observations.

Firstly, whether you are on your own or with others, take the time to really study yourself. How you are sitting, what patterns are you repeating in your behaviour that you have done before? If you did not know this person, what would you say about their attitude to life? What could they do to improve their outlook? Consider the questions we discussed in the previous section on the silent witness. Allow yourself to see your situation from an outside perspective.

Secondly, if others are involved, notice how they are reacting and behaving to the current situation. What do you sense that they are feeling? What are they thinking and feeling about you and how you are acting? See things from their perspective. If you need to, float into their body and literally see, hear and feel what they are experiencing. How does that change your perception of the situation?

Remember as a silent witness, you can get up close and personal with the situation. You are not becoming emotionally involved. You are simply making objective observations.

Finally, once you have looked at the situation from at least one of these perspectives, open your eyes and take out your note pad. Make a specific list of how the person that you were observing (you) could change his or her own self talk, attitude, perception, physiology and interaction with others. Create at least three different actions that are based on a different perception for you to immediately apply for the next 10 days. Whenever the opportunity arises, take a minute to stop what you are doing and be a silent witness to the moment and change the way you look at your current situation. Repeat this again and again to make perception change a habit.

The Movie Buff – In this role you are an avid movie watcher sitting in the cinema on your own. As a movie buff you settle into the chair and in front of you there is a massive cinema screen. The movie running today at the cinema is My Life.

This approach involves you distancing yourself from the situation you are in. To change your perception of the situation in the movie you have a set of easy-to-use controls in your hand. You have the ability to fast forward and rewind. You can make it bigger, smaller, louder, quieter or more or less colourful. You can do anything you wish with the movie. It is your life that you are watching so you can zoom in, pause, distort and change at any time. You can even change the main character's role and perception in the movie.

For example, let's imagine a person on the screen (you) is a business owner and the business is struggling. You might choose to introduce some additional characters in the movie that can help the main character. By doing this, you are introducing the idea into your own mind of people you can bring in to help you overcome your current situation. You may decide to speed the character up and make them more energetic and enthusiastic and see what the result is in the movie. You may decide to give the main character slightly comic features, making them smile more and do silly things. As you make these tweaks, fast-forwarding and rewinding, trying different approaches to the movie, you will start to have a different sense of how the situation could change. You can do the same in the area of relationships, parenting, career and health – in any area you choose.

Some essential things to play with include different endings to the movie, making the colour brighter and the sound louder. Change your character and personality and the mental outlook of the main character to see how that would impact the movie.

This may seem like an odd exercise, however I use this on many occasions both for myself and with my clients and I have found it to be extremely effective. Remember the goal here is to give yourself a different perception of your world and your current situation.

The Time Traveller – I am sure that you have heard the phrase that it is easy to make a judgment in hindsight. Each of us is able to look back in time to an occasion when we probably could have made different decisions in our lives. I am sure that you would agree that had you done this in any area of your life, that your current circumstances would be different today. It is this very principle that I would like you to apply here.

No matter what your circumstances are today, at this moment, the reality is that in five years' time you'll be in a different place in your life – this is an unquestionable truth. You and I have the ability to travel out in our minds, to a point in time in the future and look back at today. If we were to do this, it would be no different to sitting here right now, whilst reading this book and reflecting on something that happened a few years ago. So let me explain the process.

Time Travel – Stage 1

I would like you to imagine that you are a time traveller with an optimistic perception of the world. You have the ability to go forward in time and see an exciting future and all the steps that you took in order to get there. Allow yourself to relax back and ideally close your eyes, as you do so, imagine that you are in your own time machine and you set the date to two years from today. When you turn the dial and press the Time Travel button, you will move rapidly into the future. During this process your senses become magnified.

Remember what we have already spoken about previously – you create your own reality. Therefore, release any potential blocks and allow this process to take place. You are a Master Time Traveller, so you can choose where and when you wish to arrive. In a matter of seconds, you arrive at your ideal location, two years from today.

It is important that you establish a strong, clear, vibrant and positive image of this place. You are in the future and so whatever is happening right now in the present is now two years in the past – you have moved on. You feel totally different; your life has changed in so many incredibly positive ways.

At this stage I would like you to get your pad of paper ready and your pen poised to write. Now, as you look around at what you see I want you to notice:

> *How do you look and feel in this new positive environment?*
> *What is difference about your health and energy?*
> *What is the home like that you are living in?*
> *How much are you earning, saving and investing?*
> *Who are you with and how is that relationship?*
> *What are you passionate about in life at that time?*

As part of this experience it is vital that you allow yourself to connect emotionally with your future at that moment in time. In reality, two years from today you will not have any of the same emotions that you are experiencing now. In other words, you will have become disassociated from today's experience. You will still remember it but because you will have carried out the exercise for changing your perception then you will have turned the experience into a positive learning.

Time Travel – Stage 2

Your time machine can record everything in full colour and surround sound and so you can rewind it to any point in time along your journey of growth. Starting from the point two years in the future when everything has changed for you, press the 'slow rewind' button and retrace the path you took to get to that amazing place from where you were two years before. In other words, you are 24 months in the future and now begin to step backwards in time to say 22 months and have a look at what life looked like at that point. What activities and actions were you doing in order for your life to be so dramatically different? Continue to do this and you will see exactly what steps and changes you would have taken to achieve this amazing new life. The time travel process is literally allowing you to see what you need to do now to move forward.

You may not be able to fill in all the blanks along the way; however, you will certainly have a strong sense of clarity on what things would need to have happened in order for you to have reached that point. The diagram above gives some idea based on a person starting out at zero months with a financial crisis and not being able to buy their first home.

Make notes, capture the steps and use this as a guide to moving forward today, tomorrow and over the next six to 12 months. If you wish to go out further into the future you can, the choice is yours.

Responsibility (PROD)

Think about how often you hear people in relationships or in their jobs and businesses blaming other people for the circumstances they are experiencing rather than taking responsibility for what happened. The problem with blaming something or someone else is that we give our inner power to that person or thing. Have you ever heard any of these?

> *It is my wife's fault; she was always nagging me when I got home from work*
>
> *I cannot start a new business because of the recession*
>
> *I am always in debt because my boss does not pay me enough money*
>
> *The reason I am overweight and unfit is because my gym closes too early*
>
> *My boyfriend/girlfriend has lost interest in me and that's why I don't make any effort*

The fact is that we have all done it at some point in our lives. What's more dangerous is if we live in this place on a consistent and regular basis. The cycle of blame can be vicious and ultimately leads to a very low energy existence.

Lack of responsibility means lack of control of your circumstances which means you now become a victim of circumstances. Subconsciously, when a person becomes a victim they become disempowered and apathy sets in. This then leads to excuses being made and the cycle continues.

The first step to this process is to simply accept that what has happened has happened. You cannot change the past. You can learn from the past, but you cannot change it. If you keep hanging on to it, it will eat you alive. I was speaking at a Rich Dad Education event recently and an Indian gentleman approached me. His face looked heavy and stressed. He looked like he had been in pain for a long time. He had dark lines underneath his eyes, he had a permanent frown on his face and he could barely look me in the eye. Over the past 10 years, he had lost close to £1 million worth of investments and money due to a rift between himself and his ex-wife. He was carrying all this pain, blame and loss everywhere he went. Although he said he was positive, actually he wasn't. Blame quietly crept into every conversation that we had. I had a sense that it was hanging heavily on his heart and he was not prepared to take any responsibility for what happened.

In the case of this gentleman, until he is prepared to let go of what happened and take back control by taking responsibility for what happened, he is never going to move forward. If fact, that stress has the potential to cause him long-term health problems.

This is not about feeling guilty or taking the blame. This is about accepting responsibility for the choices and decisions that you have made. You must say to yourself, "I made certain decisions that have led me to this point in my life. I take full responsibility for that and I take back control of and responsibility for every decision I make in the future". When I went through my divorce, I had to do exactly this.

There have been a couple of occasions when I have had to do the same thing with decisions I have made in business or with the choice of my business partners.

Ask yourself this question – what can you take responsibility for right now. Empower yourself so that nobody else can influence how you feel – the choice is yours.

The Solution Is Simple

Take responsibility for everything you do. Take responsibility for the decisions you make, the actions that you take and the errors that you make. Take responsibility for how you are feeling about an emotionally difficult situation you may be in right now. Take responsibility for your failures, temporary set-backs and equally take responsibility for your successes.

Ownership (PROD)

Often what can happen is that you will feel like you have more ownership in some areas of your life than others. Recognising this tends to drive us towards wanting to improve the areas where we feel less ownership. The fact that you are reading this book suggests to me that this is likely to be the case for you. What many people do is to subconsciously release control of the areas that they feel weaker in and doing so, release ownership. In doing this, what you are effectively saying to the universe and those around you is that you can't control this part of your life. That in turn drives you back into the Victim role.

I truly believe that we are connected at an energetic level to a greater universe and that we attract things to us based on our beliefs and the intention we put out into the world. My experience has been that in order to align with such incredible resources and energy we must create the space in our lives to allow great things to happen. Therefore, by taking conscious ownership of what you do and trusting that you will be guided in the right direction as you step through your challenges, you will attract so many new opportunities to change. This trust walks hand-in-hand with ownership; it is about trusting yourself, those around you that will cross your path when you need them and a universe of infinite possibility.

It is quite easy to identify the areas where you probably feel a lesser degree of ownership. The list below encompasses the key areas that our lives can be grouped into. Simply look down the list and on a scale of one to ten, rate your level of happiness and contentment in each of these areas and enter the number in the box next to each area. Ten means you are completely happy and one being thoroughly unhappy. This is a simple but effective tool that works effectively to focus you in which area needs work.

☐ Health	☐ Spiritual
☐ Money & Wealth	☐ Family
☐ Career & Business	☐ Fun & Adventure
☐ Relationships	

The closer you get to one on the scoring system the lesser your degree of ownership is in this area. The reality is that you must now accept absolute ownership of each of these areas irrespective of how happy or sad you feel about them. By accepting full ownership of who you are, what has happened to you and how you show up in each area, you are then able to take responsibility for each one. When you truly take full ownership of a specific area of your life it will be an enlightening and empowering moment. This simple act then means that you can start to take full responsibility for what happens in this area of your life. You own it, nobody else and you are responsible for which direction to take it.

> Focus on you. Take ownership of your life. Resolve your challenges and grow and in doing so you will create attraction and others will come to you anyway.

Decision Making (PRO*D*)

As a public speaker and entrepreneur, I get to witness the decision process of thousands of people. Often during my seminars the clients attending have the opportunity to invest in themselves in order to attend more advanced educational classes. The reality is that in order to do this they have to make a decision as to whether they are prepared to invest more money in themselves. Under these circumstances most people's true decision-making process emerges. I have been through the same decision-making process many times over the years when being an attendee at different seminars myself.

I generally observe two types of people:

The first type of person is someone who is absolutely committed and passionate about making significant life changes. They completely understand the need to grow and develop. These people fully understand the value of the education and how it can help them on the path to better health, better relationships, business, finance or financial freedom. They do not negotiate their future or make excuses or listen to the negative 'stuff' others put on them. They act on their passion and focus on the process of growth. I have been one of these people all of my life. When I see something that I know will help me and my family I go with my heart and intuition and then I act. I truly believe that this is one of the key reasons for my success.

The second type of person philosophically understands the need to continue their education. They know that they really should invest in themselves and get the education necessary to help them achieve their goals. However, this second type of person is not committed to their ultimate purpose. They think in their head rather than from a passionate place in their heart. They start to rationalise ('rational lies') why they cannot or should not invest in themselves at this moment in time. Often their focus is on money and cost. Ironically, that is the very reason they need to re-educate themselves, in order to create a new vehicle that allows them the ability to create more wealth, health, abundance and personal growth. Worse still, they go and talk to others who are not in that environment, who have not grown, who listen to stories that are written on the internet or possibly in the media that may not necessarily be true. And so they do not proceed, they do not grow.

What is even more interesting is when you see couples making a decision related to money. Often, one partner of that couple is extremely focused and decisive, whilst the other is indecisive and less committed. This can often create more challenges. This decision process brings a magnifying glass to a conflict of values that has probably been sitting in their relationship for many years. In fact, many people would argue that the biggest cause of divorce is due to disputes over money.

Developing the skill of being a great decision maker starts with small daily actions. How do you feel when you are around somebody in your business or your personal life that is not particularly decisive? Do you feel frustrated? Equally, when you are with someone who makes decisions clearly and rapidly without any messing around, how does that feel? Decision makers tend to attract others to them. They have a sense of certainty about them that makes them good to be around. It is a very attractive quality.

Start to become a decision-making machine. Small decisions lead to bigger decisions. Take back control of the areas of your life where you feel out of control by making more decisions in those areas.

My Five-Step Formula For Decision Making

Since my early 20s I have been aware of the times when I have been more effective with my decisions and less effective with my decisions. The reality is that not every decision we make will be the right decision. However, it has been my experience and observation that by remaining indecisive in this world we allow somebody else, or some other set of circumstances, to make the decision for us. This comes back to ownership and not taking responsibility. You learn much more by making a decision and seeing it through. If the decision does not yield you the ideal result you were looking for then you learn from it and refine your process. If the decision gives you a great result, then you can reward yourself, celebrate and make a note of how you can repeat that decision-making process in the future.

Here is a five-stage process that I use myself and have used with thousands of people over the past 20 years in my career, businesses and as a professional speaker.

1. **Define the decision clearly** – CLARITY is king here. Make sure you know exactly what the decision is that you have to make and take any other issues off the table that may be clouding your judgement. Know your preferred outcome.

2. **Establish what this decision MEANS to you.** Understand the importance of the decisions and what the possible outcomes are for each of the CHOICES you have. I suggest that you close your eyes, be a time traveller, and allow yourself to go out into the future in your mind to see what each choice would result in.

3. **Make the decision** – do this in your mind and be clear what the decision means to you.

4. **Review the decision** you have chosen and ask whether the outcome will move you towards your goal and purpose and

away from your current pain. Another question I like to ask is – *'is this decision good for me, good for my family and good for the world around me?'*

5. ***Now carry out the INNER TEST*** – close your eyes, breathe in a relaxed and deep manner and allow yourself to listen to your heart and instincts. Does this decision feel right? If not, then pause, ask yourself why, follow your instincts and go back to the start again. If YES, then act on the decision as quickly as possible and do not hesitate.

You may wish to seek the counsel of a mentor or a trusted friend to check in with. There is nothing wrong with that, but do keep your inner voice close to hand. You are the best judge of how a decision feels inside. Also, on some occasions, if the decision is being made when you are not in what I call a *centred* state, then pause and if needed reflect for a short time (not days or months) – I am talking a few hours maybe. Then if you feel the same way – act.

Most importantly, decide and act. Don't sit on the fence.

Your Ten-Day Decision Making Challenge

For the next ten days, practice being more decisive. Finish each day having made a minimum of five decisions that move you out of your current blockage and towards your vision of the future. They don't all have to be big decisions. Log them in your journal and celebrate them. The key is to act on these decisions – do something to put momentum behind whatever decision it was you made.

As we talked about in the section on procrastination, create time urgency around the decision process. Look to simplify your decision process. One way to do this is to simply ask the question 'does this action move me closer or further away from my primary goal at present?' If it does move you closer, then take action. If it doesn't then look to delegate it, move it to a more appropriate time or simply get rid of it.

Also learn to follow your gut instincts when it comes to decision-making. All too often people intellectualise the decision that has to be made even though their gut reaction was negative or positive to start with. The problem with intellectualising something is that you then start to rationalise and justify why you should or should not do the thing you are deliberating over, then it takes more time. If your instincts tell you one thing and you go against them then you may find that you are not wholeheartedly committed to seeing it through.

Your Decision To Change

So now we are at the end of Section One. My hope is that in working through this part of the book you have gained a strong understanding of what is necessary to ensure that positive change can happen. Simply being aware of the blocks that can stop your success allows you to see them if they emerge on the path ahead. I encourage you to pause and flick back over all the previous chapters, skim and absorb key points that are relevant to you. Then accept full ownership of your power and put a smile on your face because now you are about to start the Six Step Change Process – let's begin.

The Six-Step
Change Process

4 | **Step One** - Master Your Internal and External Language

Introduction

The very first step in the Six Step Change Process is the skill of mastering your self-communication skills. By doing this, you will be able to self-correct your path and continuously install positive and empowering beliefs and thoughts even in the most challenging times. It all starts with what you say and how you say it.

Although we are taught at an early age how to speak and communicate with other people, I do not believe that we are truly made aware of the incredible power and impact that words have on our subconscious. In fact, it was not really until I got into the world of personal development that I really discovered that a single word said with enough intent can change the biochemistry of your body. People spend thousands of pounds on surgery and chemical treatments in the hope that they can change their body and the way they feel. What they don't realise is that they are able to use powerful and emotional words to trigger certain thoughts which in turn activate an emotional response that results in cellular and chemical changes. No drugs or surgery needed. Based on this understanding, it makes sense that you can change your emotional state and feeling of well being by what you say to yourself and to other people.

In order to get the greatest impact from your self-communication, it requires an emotional commitment to the change you wish to experience. It requires physical activity to create momentum within your inner and outer world. It requires a true and pure intention behind what you are saying and a genuine desire for the change you are seeking to make. And, above all, it requires trust in the process and consistency in the way you language your words. Without this level of commitment, your intentions will merely be wishes that never get realized. So the key is to be committed to what you say.

Communication & The Silent Witness

Previously we have discussed the importance of being a silent witness, now I would like you to step up and become the Ultimate Communications Silent Witness. Later in this chapter we will discuss the difference between internal communication and external communication. The more insightful you become as the Ultimate Communications Silent Witness, the more articulate and empowering your words will be. I cannot stress the importance of this. You will reach a point very quickly where your ability to recognise disempowering internal and external language will be so sharp that you can change both your thought process and the external communication process in a matter of seconds.

As you start to apply your new language of communication I would like you to use the following three steps:

1. Imagine that you are sitting next to yourself and observe your actions and listen to every word that you say to yourself and to others.

2. Pay close attention to three specific things: (i) The tone, pace and the energy in your voice (ii) How you feel and hold yourself in a physical way (your physiology) and (iii) The specific words and language that you are using.

3. At a deeper level, I want you to identify the intention behind this communication. In other words, what is the core outcome of what you are saying or asking? Are you coming from a positive or

negative 'place'? Are you looking for solutions? Are you seeking empowering and enlightened answers? Are you steering the communication in such a way that you can overcome obstacles and bring out the best in you and who you are talking with?

Remember that awareness is the first major step to change. Therefore by making these observations and asking quality questions, you automatically start to recognize where your language and communication patterns are holding you back. Let's now start to drill down into the areas that really impact your communication.

Six Forms of Communication That Impact Your Life

We are going to focus you on *the language of results*. I believe there are six elements to communication and if you study and understand their power you will not only be able to master your own words, but also know how to spike destructive self-communication.

Internal Communication – internal communication takes place both at a conscious and subconscious level. At any one moment you are either consciously talking to yourself or your subconscious is processing ideas without you being aware of it. From my observations, it is this internal communication that directly influences what you ultimately say when you communicate with the outside world.

External Communication – most of what you say outwardly to people is a reflection on what you are saying to yourself internally. That is why I find it quite easy to be able to read a person's mind because their words, body language and tonality leave massive clues as to what is really going on inside their head. Although you may be able to hide some of what you are thinking, with close observation, your true thoughts will be expressed through a change in breathing, a sigh, a twitch of an eye or change in your posture. Ultimately, your body can't lie when it comes to what you really feel.

Statements – when you make a statement, you are simply saying out loud or internally what you believe about the current situation you are experiencing or observing. A statement can often lead to questions that lead to greater clarity. You make statements to yourself at an internal and external level. These statements will come from the beliefs that you currently hold about the world. Remember, irrespective of whether these statements are correct or not, if you believe them, then they are true to you.

Questions – when you ask a question of yourself it automatically creates a subconscious and conscious change in your focus. As a coach, mentor and speaker I have been privileged enough to really see the value of questions and the impact they can have on completely changing a person's perspective of the world. You not only have the ability to do this with yourself but also with other people. Let's change your focus right now with three simple questions:

Was the weather outside hot today?

What would you look like in a pair of massive purple sunglasses?

How would you feel if I gave you £50,000 to spend on yourself?

Each of these questions requires you to engage in the experience of what you have been asked about in order to answer the question. In other words, a specific question can guide you to a whole new experience in your mind without actually experiencing it. This means if you want to experience a great feeling and positive results, ask better quality questions that can produce the outcome you are looking to experience.

Desire – what I mean by desire is anything in your life that you aspire to experience, achieve, have or do. Some people refer to this as the dream, others the outcome, other people might refer to it as an aspiration. When you communicate your desire it creates attraction and when created with enough passion and intention it communicates a message to the world around you that you are on purpose and seeking help and support. Allow yourself the gift of focusing purely on what you would like to attract into your life in a graceful and open way.

Fear – through muscle testing, also known as kinesiology, fear-based communication has been shown to physically weaken the body. This is why people who communicate internally and externally in a fearful way often look physically smaller and facially distressed (frowning, tension and often drawn). When you communicate to yourself or to others from an emotional place of fear you create a negative attractive force. However, through the use of questions and a change in your self-communication, your perception of the fear that you have can be reduced or removed. In many cases when this process takes place there is a massive sense of relief, tears and in some cases vomiting or diarrhoea. This may appear extreme, but it is simply the body's way of letting go of something that has literally been suffocating it. Let's look at an example.

James's Communication Challenge

I have a client who is 27 years of age, his name is James and for the past six years he has looked after both his mother and younger brother and sister. One of his greatest challenges was that in the past several years he was going in circles in his career and felt everything that he tried outside of work to create financial security had failed.

As I listened to him for about an hour responding to my various questions, it was clear what the main problem was. James's whole language pattern, both internal and external, was fear driven. Even when he talked about what he wanted to experience, it was stated in such a way that it referred to what he did not want to experience. For example, two common statements he made were, "I simply do not want to keep setting goals and failing" and "I don't want to keep waking up in the morning feeling down and depressed about my life".

In response to the last statement, I asked him, "So what do you really want to experience every day when you wake up?" to which he replied, "I don't want to feel tired and emotionally drained". I replied, "OK James, let me ask the question a different way, what would you love to experience and feel whenever you wake up?" and he replied, "I don't want to be worried about constantly looking after my family and having to work hard in order to achieve that".

Hopefully you can see how seriously self-destructive James's external and internal communication patterns were. Even without knowing James, you and I can see that what he was saying to the outside world was a reflection of an internal battle that was going on in his heart and mind. This battle will have been a communication between his conscious and his subconscious focusing on the fear that he had about his work and his life. Even though we know that he wants a better quality of life, that is not where his focus was and language was. Hence, the statements were purely related to what he does not want to experience. This fear-based communication becomes a language of desire – sadly for James it was a desire for what he did not want and hence he was simply experiencing more and more of what he was saying and wanted to get away from. That is why things had been getting worse not better.

The Language of Results

Your goal then should be to focus your internal and external communication with a balance between questions and statements that are directed purely towards what you do want to experience and achieve (DESIRE) rather than what you don't want to achieve (FEAR). This is the language of results. When faced with a challenge, instead of using the language of fear such as 'why does this keep happening' or 'I will never find a way to do this', you must use statements that channel your internal resources to seek out a better result. For example, a statement like 'I have the resources and the people around me to help me find a solution' or 'I thrive on opportunities like this to grow and become a better person.'

This approach works – no debate, no arguments or suggestions that it is all motivational hype. It works and it does so when applied consistently and with genuine desire to attract a solution. Richard Branson, in his book *Screw It Let's Do It* talks about the fact that they call him the YES man at Virgin. I love that. He has the attitude, that yes, we can find a way to make this happen.

The same applies to questions. 'Why does this keep happening to me?' directs your subconscious and conscious mind to all the problems you are facing. Instead, simply asking 'What can I do to ensure that I create a much better result next time?' immediately puts you into a solution-directed mindset. Simplistic? Yes. Does it work? Yes. This is not about ignoring what is happening in your life which will be as real to you as anything else around you. This is about redirecting your focus to create a more resourceful emotional state.

You may find that when you really apply this approach some people who are negative and fear driven will literally get annoyed with you because all you keep doing is staying positive and looking for solutions. Have fun with this. Don't compromise your values to meet their needs. Use results-driven language and watch what happens over time.

It's All About Direction

From the above six forms of communication, there are two that can totally govern your mood and emotional state. We are going to explore these more closely. It is vital that you remember the objective behind what we are discussing. Your goal is to overcome the obstacles that lie ahead of you. Your goal is to create a more resourceful mindset and environment. Your goal is to move your life forward in a more positive direction with much more effective results.

With that in mind, the process of effective results-driven language becomes much easier. Remember, we talk to ourselves every waking hour that we are alive. This conversation is conscious, subconscious and external. Therefore, as I have said already in this chapter, you must choose your words carefully in order to get the best results.

We will focus on *Statements and Questions* and I will be asking you to review the way you use these two methods of communication. In doing so I would like you to create a section in your journal where you write down every single new empowering statement or question that is developed. It is not enough to hold them in your mind, it is vital that you write them down so that you can practice and make them habitual.

Statements

Statements are a reflection of what you are thinking and feeling. The more emotionally charged you are when you make a statement, the greater the level of belief you are likely to have in that statement. We will discover later the impact that beliefs can have on everything you say to yourself. Let me take one of my business clients as an example. Sajid has been running a business for almost 15 years, rarely taking a holiday and never increasing his own salary within his business. Here are some examples of typical statements he made when I first started working with him.

I desperately need to escape from this box

I need to find a way to stop my staff complaining

I need to be less unhappy in my role in the business

I need to get my staff to work harder and not be so lazy

I need to have more time with my family and not work so hard

In the diagram below you will see a simple illustration that shows internal and external communication. Communication to the outside world can only take place based on what occurs in the two inner circles of communication. Therefore, in Sajid's case, if we were to delve inside his mind with a microphone and listen to the communication that was taking place it is very clear that there are two very distinct patterns to his statements:

a) **Lack and Fear** – from the words he was using it is clear that he was coming from a place of fear and lack. This is apparent by certain word patterns. Whenever anybody uses the words *I need* in the description of what they are looking to achieve, it reflects a massive sense of lack in their lives. What I mean by lack is that they have a gap, a fear and a fundamental belief that there is not enough of what they are hoping to achieve. Since they believe there is not enough, it becomes a need rather than an enjoyable openhearted desire. His life was driven by fear-based need.

b) **Negative Focus** – hopefully you will have noticed that every statement that Sajid made reflected what he did not want to experience. For example, "I need to be *less unhappy* in my role in the business." His focus here was on being less unhappy rather than wanting to 'feel happy and excited' in his business. In fact, it became clear that this form of language crossed over into virtually everything he spoke about. On a physical level, his face looked aged and he wore a continuous frown. This is not surprising bearing in mind that he was always focusing on what he did not want to experience.

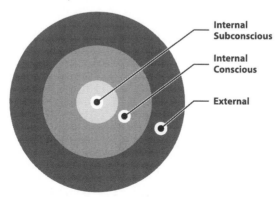

I was able to help Sajid make a rapid and massive change in his attitude and language patterns by simply focusing on the above two areas. Try this on yourself. Any time you find yourself using the word need in relation to something that you would like to achieve or attract, then you should immediately rephrase the statement. Examples of what you could use to replace the word need are listed below:

Old: *I need to have new experiences*

New: ***I would love to experience...***

Old: *I need to make more money*

New: ***It will be fantastic when I develop my new business and receive more income***

Old: *I need to find a partner that understands me 100%*

New: ***I'm excited about meeting a wonderful partner and getting to know them***

Old: *I need to find a way to forget this tragic loss in my life*

New: ***I am blessed to have known this person and know that I will always carry a part of them with me as I find a new path in my life.***

Statements should be repeated on an internal level in a consistent and regular way. It also helps to repeat them out loud with a smile and a deep sense of gratitude. If, for example, you are single and wanting to start a new relationship, get comfortable with saying to yourself that you are excited about meeting a wonderful partner. Whenever you are quietly relaxing and meditating allow these words to pass through your mind and into your focus.

As you allow your subconscious and conscious minds to quietly repeat these words at different times during the day, you'll find it much easier to articulate them when you're speaking to other people. What you are really doing here is reprogramming the language that you have previously used. In order for this to be a habit, you must do it often and keep repeating the process until the new habit is formed. Don't stop after a week – keep going, again and again. It needs to become second nature.

As simple as this may sound, it works. Don't complicate it. Don't underestimate it because of its simplicity. Trust in the process and trust in yourself. Start to identify all of the statements that you currently make coming from a place of fear and lack and then reword them. Don't look for immediate results and don't monitor things all the time. Allow your mind to relax into this new way of thinking and communicating. It may take longer for you than someone else – or it may happen very quickly. The results will become apparent in the way you act and communicate with others. Walk first, then jog and eventually you will be running with a whole new form of daily statements that empower you in everything you do.

Questions

Whilst statements are essentially an expression of what you believe at that moment, *questions* are the searchlight of your subconscious.

Without doubt, one of the biggest discoveries in my life was the power of questions and how they can impact the way we think. This may sound like a bold statement, however for almost two and half decades I have been using different questioning techniques (internal and external) to produce amazing result. In fact it was during my Ph.D. that I truly understood the importance of questions. My Ph.D. supervisor, Prof Stuart Littlejohn, always encouraged me to ask searching questions that looked at a problem in a completely different way. Throughout my Ph.D. this became one of my mantras, 'Ask a different question, try it a different way and look for a different result'. What if this happened? What if that happened? What is another way to solve this problem? Who could I speak to in order to make this more efficient? I became a questioning machine, honing my skill to ask more powerful questions each time.

There is one single thing I would like you to remember about questions. Questions have the ability to change your focus in an instant. Do you remember the last time you were laying out in the sun slowly drifting away into a lovely sleep? Whilst lying in the heat, how did it feel? What were you wearing? Were you on your own or with a loved one? Were you lying on the grass or on the beach?

Notice that that every new question I asked resulted in a shift of your focus. You will recall that we talked about this in previous chapters. In fact, with a series of questions you can actually take yourself on a journey to any moment in time and to any experience in time that you have had or potentially could have in the future.

So how does this work?

Whether you are engaged in an internal conversation or an external conversation with somebody else, when a question is asked it immediately moves to your conscious mind. That means you cannot avoid having to focus on the question itself. The same thing can happen when you have a specific thought. The thought brings the idea into your conscious mind and then you have to focus on it. At that point your mind then starts to analyze what the question means.

In order to answer the question, even if you do not want to answer it, you have to first think about what the question is asking you. For example, let me ask you how would you look if you were wearing a bright pink hat on your head? Depending on your own method of processing, you will either:

a) Visualize the hat

b) Internalize the thought or feeling of a hat (feel what it would be like)

c) Hear the question and then imagine what it would be like to wear the hat

There are variations on this, and sometimes people say to me that they don't or can't actually visualize a question. However, when pushed harder for their specific process it always results in them having created an image of the answer to the question in order for them to decide whether they wish to answer or not.

The key point here is that in responding to a question you will first have had to put your focus on what the question is, what it means to you and how it would look. *That is a shift of focus and you cannot avoid it.* This makes questioning a very powerful process.

Why is this so important? Start by looking at the following diagram.

We've already established in our previous chapter that what you place your thoughts on results in an emotional response in your body. Another way of saying this is 'what you focus on with enough intensity can affect the way you feel'. Therefore by default, if a question can change your focus, it can change a thought pattern, which in turn can change the way you feel. Now imagine that you have the ability to ask very specific and directed questions at any moment in your life. If you do this, you are able to shift your focus the same way you would do if you were using a torch or a searchlight to find something at night.

So any moment in time when you are feeling overwhelmed, frustrated or you simply don't know which direction to go then questions can be used to narrow your focus down to a specific set of answers that will, one hundred percent be able to move you forward.

The skill is to switch between broader questions to give you a larger perspective and much sharper questions to focus you in on the real result that you are looking to achieve. You goal is to become a *Question Master.*

How to Become a Question Master

To become a Question Master is not difficult. It simply takes practice and most importantly, it requires you to be clear on what the end result is that you are looking for. So let's explore the process. The only way that you will truly be able to master this is to apply it on a consistent and daily basis. When I personally started to use this process, I was shocked at how rapidly my subconscious mind changed the way it communicated with my conscious mind. Conversations with other people became clearer and sharper. I was able to get to results quicker. I was able to filter out the wood from the trees. When people around me were confused and unclear about what to do, I was able to rapidly help them and myself get clarity. When necessary, I was able to detach myself from the emotion of a situation in order to get an objective result. You will be able to do exactly the same.

The Question Master Process

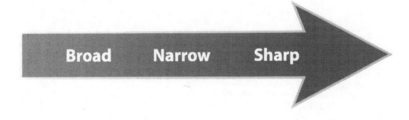

Interestingly, in writing this book, I chose to take on my coach, Mindy, to help me accelerate the process. I also knew that with her experience, she would be able to ask me specific questions that maybe I was unaware of, in order to help me get clarity and more rapid results. In the very same way, my clients use me to help them get clarity in specific areas of their lives.

In summary then, you start with broad questions, you narrow down the questions to gain clarity and then ask very specific questions to get a sharp and accurate answer.

An Essential Rule of Questioning

As you move down the process of narrowing your questions, it is essential to remember that the intention behind the questions must be driven by a positive mindset. Negatively driven questions produced negatively driven responses. As simple and obvious as it may sound, it still surprises me just how many people phrase their questions from a negative perspective.

Remember to stay in the moment and to be a silent witness. Check in with yourself and ask if these questions are coming from a place of fear and lack. If they are, then stand up, take a deep breath and put a smile on your face and refocus. Anger, fear and frustration are low vibration energies and if questions come from this place in your mind, it will be like fanning the flames of a fire and putting more wood on at the same time. You will create more fear. So ask positively directed questions that seek solutions.

Broad Questions

The starting point in any situation is to ask broad questions. Remember the question needs to enable you to get a positive overview of what you are trying to achieve. If you are in a relationship that is struggling and you are feeling hopeless and directionless then you need to ask a broad question first. This might include questions like 'Am I still committed to making this relationship work?' or 'How can I help my partner understand how much I really want to make this relationship work?' or 'What are the inspiring reasons, in my heart, for me to work on re-igniting my relationship?'

Make the questions broad enough to allow more than one positive answer to come out.

If you are currently facing financial challenges and can't see a way out, you might ask questions like 'What are the key areas I know I need to work on in order to improve my finances?' or 'In the area of my expenses, which monthly items can I start to reduce over the next few months' or 'What skills and opportunities can I start to look at in order to increase my income?'

Remember that the objective at this stage is not to get specific. Instead you are looking for several avenues down which to take your narrowing sharper questions. In many cases, such as the financial example above, you may have chosen to go down each of the paths that have been identified by the broader question. For example, a broad question relating to your expenses would lead to more specific questions relating to how much? When? How often? And why things are spent?

Having gained clarity with your expenses, you then go back to the top again and start down another area of finances like debt management for example. Here are some examples of broader questions:

What do I believe about money?

What does it mean to be healthy?

How do I know I have a problem in my relationship?

Who are the people involved in this situation?

When do I feel stressed about my finances?

What would I like to be different in my life 12 months from today?

Narrow Through To Sharper Questions

In the back of your mind I would like you to remember the mantra 'keep drilling down, keep drilling down, keep drilling down'. The broader questions enable us to get the overview, the narrow and sharp questions take us right to the heart of the issue. One of my previous clients had an obsession with his poor health. He constantly made statements like 'I feel crappy, I need more energy but can't find any. I just feel really pi –ed off with myself for not doing anything about it'. I jumped right in with a broader, more positive question and asked him, "How would you like to feel and look?" This led to a broad description of how he would like to feel, the shape of his body, the energy levels he would have and the clarity of thought he would have in his mind.

Had my client at any time responded with statements back to what he does not want to look and feel like, I would have had to *refocus* him with a slightly narrower positive question to make sure the statement that he made were geared towards what he wanted to experience rather than what he wanted to avoid.

I then narrowed down the questions: "In order to feel that fit and healthy what needs to happen for you next?" and "what would you need to change in your diet in order to look and feel the way you have just described?" Notice also that the questions were aimed at creating *action-oriented* answers. His response to these questions was, "I would like to be eating healthier and less cooked food. Plus I know I am ready to give up soda-based drinks."

Hopefully you can see what is happening here. This is a process that you can use on yourself anytime by making the questions tighter and more specific. In the case of my client I was then able to take this to another level and dig deeper and be more specific. "Great, so specifically what types of food and drink would you like to eat to be healthier." When I went through this process with my client he was able to list in detail different food types that he knew he wanted to eat. Having identified this I then asked him specific questions relating to when he would be doing this and how he would be doing this.

During this process of gaining absolute clarity there must to be a timeframe and a mechanism for providing the solution. As a reminder then, each question should help you get closer to the specific answer. You can do this using questions starting with the following:

a) **What**

b) **When**

c) **Where**

d) **How**

Remember that you have reached this stage in the process because you are motivated enough to make a significant changes in your life. Therefore the reason or the why you are doing this has already been established in your mind. However, if for some reason you do not have to have a high degree of motivation to make a specific change in what you are doing, then an important question to add to the above list should include 'e) *Why* is this important to me'.

Here are examples of narrowing questions:

What specifically am I not prepared to settle for any more?

What are the things I love most about my partner?

In which exact area of my finances do I have the greatest pain?

What is the most important activity in the next 48hrs that I have to complete?

What charity will I support this year?

How would I like to look when I have achieved my health goals?

Where do I truly want my business to be in 2 years' time?

Internal – External – Internal Questions and Statements

I would like to finish this chapter by describing the process that is continually taking place when you are talking to yourselves and others. I often refer to this as the internal-external-internal cycle. This is a cycle of questions and answers that I have illustrated in the diagram below. At any one moment in time when you are having an internal dialogue with yourself it will have been triggered by either an external circumstance or an internal thought. For example, you hear announcement about your company downsizing and you immediately ask yourself the question 'Does that mean I will be made redundant?' This is your *reaction* to external circumstances.

Alternatively, you may simply be sitting at home relaxing at the end of a normal working day and you reflect on the current economic climate and, as a result, you ask yourself the question, 'what if my company has to downsize because of the recession?' This is not a reaction to circumstance but simply a thought that comes from *within*.

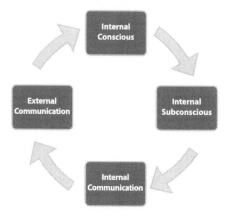

You and I talk to ourselves all day long. You might smile, but it's true. It is a conversation of statements and questions being made at lightning speed. The final result, whether it be positive or negative, ends up back in your conscious mind and then through your words and your body language expressed to the external world.

Although many people do not consider the conscious mind to be as powerful as the subconscious mind, I believe that most people simply do not understand how to direct it to optimise its power. You can switch your conscious mind on and direct it any time. In this respect the fastest and most effective way to allow your conscious and subconscious mind to align in a positive way is through:

1. *Questions that get rapid results*

2. *Positive declarations made in the present*

Questions that get rapid results

I realize that you have a unique set of circumstances. However, I would like to provide you with some typical questions that need to go into your Question Master toolkit. If they are not completely appropriate to you then modify them in alignment with your current situation. Your goal here is to create at least five empowering and laser-sharp questions.

> *What lessons can I learn from this situation to avoid it happening again in my life?*
>
> *What is the most significant thing I can take away from this that will help me grow?*
>
> *If I were to assume that I had every resource available to solve this problem, how would I solve it?*
>
> *If I were to really work at this relationship to make it exciting and passionate, what would I specifically need to do in order to reconnect with my partner?*
>
> *If I was completely happy in my current career right now, what would I be doing and where would I be doing it?*
>
> *What are three powerful characteristics of the person who inspires me most and how can I emulate them?*

You should be able to hear yourself internally asking very specific questions about your circumstances. One of those questions must include a connection with another human being. For example, 'who can I speak to in order to get help to resolve this situation?'

This is a skill that can be developed so don't get too concerned if you don't get it right the first time. Practice, and whatever the results are, adjust the questions and then go again.

Declarations that reinforce positive beliefs

For decades, authors and speakers in the world of personal development have shared with their readers and audiences the importance of positive affirmations and declarations. So I am not going to re-invent the wheel here. However, I do want you to understand the importance of using declarations. Note the emphasis here on declarations.

When you make a declaration, you are effectively making a statement of fact. Irrespective of whether or not it is currently true in your life, by its very expression you are reinforcing the belief that you wish to have. You and I have been programmed all of our life by external beliefs put upon us by other people. Whether those beliefs were correct or not, true or false, we subconsciously will have adopted many of them. So now it is time to crush the ones that do not serve you, which we will do in Chapter 7. Then you re-install a new set of statements and beliefs that will serve you in a much better way.

Declarations carried out on a regular and consistent basis using internal and external global language will help make this happen. It works. And if something works, then the only thing to really do is take it on and fully experience it for yourself. The statements need to be made with high energy and passion, not monotone and whispered whilst you are hiding in the toilet. Let them out with enthusiasm. Here are a few examples of *declarations*:

> *"I am a confident, friendly and enthusiastic person and people enjoy talking to me"*
>
> *"I attract opportunities to me every day"*
>
> *"I value myself, my services and I have the ability to create wealth by helping others"*
>
> *"I am a loving, passionate and attractive woman/man"*
>
> *"I am prepared to do whatever it takes to live a full and exciting life"*
>
> *"I eat food that energises me in a natural, organic way and I enjoy the process of getting healthier every day"*

I carry such declarations around with me in my wallet; I repeat them out loud at different times of the day in different circumstances. Dump your pride and the social conditioning that says you cannot do this. Negative people do this all the time. They repeat the bad news they have read in the papers, they tell you what you are bad at or how crappy their life is. Other people do it without realising it – they make statements that are simply declarations. It is your chance to create a whole series of declaration that you want in your life now. Try it when you are driving, in the shower, having breakfast, jogging, working out – you could even try when you are in the heat of passion but do be careful what you say!

Declarations magnify the intent that you are putting out to the universe. They tell your body at a cellular level what you want to attract and they tell your conscious and sub-conscious mind what level of communication should be taking place. Finally, they tell people around you what and how you are and what you want to show up on a daily basis – it sets the rules for how you want people to communicate with you. This will result in you attracting more positively guided people.

5 | Step Two
- Revaluing Your Life

Introduction

The next step in the change process is the re-alignment of your core values that make up the very essence of who you are and how you show up in the world. Remembering that I have a commitment to help you apply what you are reading in this book; I would like to urge you to dig deeper in this chapter. This next step of your change process cannot happen through osmosis. This is the furnace and you need to put yourself into the fire so that you can reforge who you are and how you want to show up in the world. Yes, I know that sounds dramatic, but that is what I want it to be – a dramatic awakening and significant change for you. So even if you feel you may have done a similar exercise like this before, do it again. And then do it again if you have to until you have cleared out the 'old junk' that has been holding you back and re-forge who you want to be. This next step in the process is one hundred percent about change.

> The way you are feeling right now about your life and about who you are, is purely down to four things – your core beliefs about the world, the core values by which you live your life, the conditions that govern whether your experiences are good or bad, and the clarity you have about your true purpose in life.

Since you have come this far, I will assume that you are committed to coming further down the rabbit hole with me. So let us continue and my hope is that my previous statement will become clear to you.

Deeper Down The Rabbit Hole

You are now ready to take a good look inside at what makes you who you are today. What is fascinating about this part of the process is that many of your core values will have been formed by observation, experience and reading or in most cases imparted to you from those around you in your earlier years – in particular your parents. At the very centre of who you are lie two components of your make-up as shown below.

These two elements are intimately linked to each other – the core values can only be achieved when the value conditions are met. Let me explain. Imagine that you value happiness a lot in your life. In other words, happiness is a value that is important to you. In order for you to feel happy, you will have a set of sub-conscious conditions that tell you when you are or are not happy. It is that simple. If the conditions for being happy are not met, then you are sad. That is the relationship between Values and Value Conditions.

Conditions. If you can consciously assess and, where necessary, re-align the values you wish to live your life by and then review and put in place a set of easy-to-satisfy conditions for these new rules – then you will find that you see and experience the world in a completely different and positive way. It is an incredibly powerful experience and you are about to do it.

What is your real Value?

The values by which you experience and live your life play a massive role in the choices you make and the people you associate with. Values sit right alongside beliefs, purpose and conditions on your journey ahead.

There are different definitions for what is meant by a Value. The *Oxford English Dictionary* classifies 'Values' as 'beliefs about what is right and wrong and what is important in life'. Another definition I read elsewhere is 'beliefs of a person or social group in which they have an emotional investment'.

I would like to suggest that a value is simply an emotional state or experience that you put an importance on in your life. The example we explored above related to the feeling of happiness. If you attached a high level of importance to feeling happy and you believe that you are a happy person, then happiness becomes a Core Value. When a person has *Happiness* as a Core Value, it is reflected in their daily actions with a positive, fun attitude. In other words they live and show up in life by this value.

Equally, if you like the emotional feeling of being successful and you place a strong emphasis on this in your life then achievement or success would become one of the Core Values you live by.

We each have many different levels of values, some with a greater importance to us than others. The ones I want you to focus on are your Core Values. These are so important that if you meet someone of a totally opposite set of Core Values you may subconsciously create an instant disliking towards that other person.

Let's imagine that you massively value the feeling of being healthy, so much so that health is a Core Value to you. That would mean that your beliefs around health would also be very strong. If you were to meet and talk with someone who has no regard or respect for their health, and in fact has a slight attitude towards overly healthy people, you would immediately have a sense of resistance to this person.

Remember that in the opposite way, they would resist your values which are opposite to what they believe. This type of encounter is therefore a battle of values and these two people may not get on unless they find some common values. Often, when you do not connect with another person, it is not so much them that you don't like, but rather your subconscious mind finds a conflict with their values and hence you switch off or have a sense of dislike towards them without sometimes knowing why.

Values Conflict

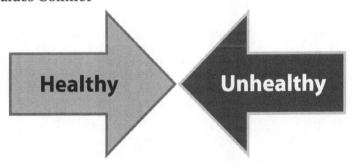

Very often, when we start to feel frustrated and unhappy in an area of our life it is because we are internally experiencing a conflict of Core Values in the area that we are unhappy. For example, if you have a core belief that you want to *feel free and in control* of your life, then a Core Value would be 'Freedom to Choose' or another word for that might be 'independence'. If you are stuck in a job and working long hours for a company that does not reward you, you are going to feel trapped. This feeling of being trapped is the exact opposite to feeling *independent* and immediately there is a misalignment with your job and your Core Value of independence.

The vital step that you have to take is to get clarity on what your Core Values are. Once you bring this into your consciousness, you are able to notice which things in your life do not align with these values that make you who you are. It sounds simple and it is – but it takes some work, discipline and emotional soul searching. So let's get cracking.

What Do You Value Most?

When I first did this exercise it took me at least half a day plus lots of intense soul searching. So this can sometimes be an emotionally challenging process and is often done well when working with the support of a trusted friend. Treat this exercise as seriously as life and death, because that is exactly what it is. If you don't live by an uplifting set of Core Values you will literally die through a life without passion, fun, health and excitement. So let's shake the tree, get rid of any bad apples that you don't want and plant some new seeds.

Abraham Maslow was a prolific American psychologist who developed a model for human behaviour that he called Humanistic Psychology. It was from this model that he developed the Hierarchy Of Human Needs. The needs can also be related to six basic Core Values and include physiological needs (oxygen, water etc), security needs (safety and stability), love and belonging needs (friends, family etc), the esteem needs (respect from others, confidence etc) and finally self-actualising needs (growth beyond oneself and giving). He identified that these core needs or values were essential to the very existence of a human being.

So why do I share this with you. Well, firstly to let you know that what I am covering here is nothing new and yet so few people really understand it. Secondly, I wanted to expand on these basic human values so that you see that there are many other needs that you as a person attach just as much importance to. In fact, in many cases you may have other values that you hold so dear, that to compromise them would make you physically sick, angry or even depressed. To help you fully understand your Core Values I am going to ask you to do an exercise.

An Essential Core Values Exercise

Let me give you some examples of typical Core Values, they are in no particular order. As you read the list I want you to observe and notice how strongly you feel about each one.

☐	Happiness	☐	Learning
☐	Health	☐	Integrity
☐	Passion	☐	Thoughtfulness
☐	Love	☐	Success
☐	Honesty	☐	Competitiveness
☐	Achievement	☐	Joyfulness
☐	Intelligence	☐	Contribution
☐	Being The Best	☐	Security
☐	Sharing	☐	Significance
☐	Creativity	☐	Fun
☐	Gratitude	☐	Being Right
☐	Achievement	☐	Recognition
☐	Wisdom	☐	Acceptance
☐	Power	☐	Control
☐	Spirituality	☐	Pride

Read the value out loud and ask yourself, from the heart, how important it is for you to experience this emotion in your life.

In the box to the left of the value I would like you to score 1 to 5 based on the following:

Rating	Your Level of Connection with the Core Value
1	No emotional connection
2	You are aware of this value but are generally indifferent to it
3	You believe this value to be important and do adopt it sometimes
4	You have strong connection and you believe this is part of your essential make up
5	You have a very strong connection with this value – this is definitely part of who you are

The important thing here is not to intellectualise the experience. Allow your body and heart to react rather than your head. A way to do this is to take a deep breath, read the value, then close your eyes and say it out loud and feel the word. Notice how it feels and allow the level of connection to flow through you and then record the rating. Give each one a rating from 1 to 5 in the box next to the value.

In addition to rating the above values, the next stage is to take out your journal and list out as many other values (aside from those above) that you are aware of that you feel show up in the way you currently live your life. Please note that this is about how you live now and not how you want to live (we will come to that a little later in the chapter). To help identify any other important values, you may want to try answering the following question. What emotion (value) would you do anything to be able to experience? Naturally, having written down additional values to those above, then you need to rate these on a scale of 1 to 5 in the same way.

I believe that probably less that 1% of the population actually do this exercise, so once you have done it I would like to congratulate you since so few people do it. Well done. So what happens next?

You are now going to create your own hierarchy of values by working through all the above values and the additional ones you wrote down. If you take the time to do this, you will discover exactly what the top three values are that have governed your life. Once you have done that, then we will look at which ones need to be re-ordered!

My Hierarchy of Values

When I first did this exercise I was at a point in my life where I felt like I was chasing 'success' all the time. I seemed to leap at virtually every opportunity, I felt frustrated that it was not happening fast enough and annoyed with myself that having worked so hard to get a PhD that I still had not reached the levels of financial success I had originally wanted in my career. I wanted to experience different things in life, to travel and try different adventures but my work and business focus seemed to dominate everything. On top of that, I was not looking after my health as much as I wanted to and I had started to neglect my relationship with my then girlfriend who is now my fiancée. I was positive in many areas of my life but very frustrated in a few others.

So I listed out and placed in order my hierarchy of values at that moment in time. You can see the order below. Note that this is in order of most importance – No. 1 being the most dominant value in my life at that time. I have only listed the top eight; however, the original exercise included some 15 to 20 values.

Rohan's Original Hierarchy of Values

1. Achievement
2. Love and passion
3. Financial freedom
4. Fulfilment
5. Excitement and fun
6. Recognition
7. Contribution
8. Being desirable

It is important to note here that you can literally make an assessment of a person and how they show up in the world by looking at their hierarchy of needs. In particular, when you look at their top three to five Core Values you can pretty much confirm what their main focus is on a day-to-day basis. If that person's number one value is extremely strong and becomes a dominating emotional focus, then virtually every other value can be ignored in order that they protect and experience life according to this one primary value.

If you look at my original hierarchy of values you can start to see why my life was operating as it was. Two of my top three needs were focused on success, achievement and financial independence. Health did not figure in any of the top eight Core Values, which is why I was feeling unhealthy. Another reason this was frustrating is because I have always been fit and healthy and it had previously been in the top three of my Core Values. You can also see why my relationship was starting to feel strained because the success-oriented values were dominating love and passion.

Since the process I went through in leading up to this exercise was also very intense, when I sat with the piece of paper in front of me and looked at my list of top core needs, I actually cried. It became black and white to me why I was continuing the same pattern of chasing so many different opportunities and feeling frustrated. I also realised that if I continued on this path it would probably end up in severe health challenges and a broken relationship. That alone was enough leverage (pain) for me to make whatever changes were needed.

Identifying Your Existing Hierarchy of Values

Okay, now it is your turn. In your journal I would like you to select the values from the list that you have just created that you scored 3 or above. Rewrite this list out, leaving anything with a 1 or 2 rating aside. You do not have to worry about what order to place them in at this stage. So now you should have listed, in your journal, a set of values that you have previously given an emotional association of 3, 4 or 5.

Now you are going to go through a procedure of sorting them in order of priority to give you a list like the one I had. To do this you can use a number of different sorting approaches.

+ *An intuitive process of which ones feel the most important*

+ *Assessing them by how much time you are spending experiencing each value*

+ *Comparing them two at a time and working through the list*

The last approach is one I find very effective. I used to use a similar sorting process during my PhD to identify possible correlations in the data I was researching. It is fast and effective and ideal when used for really drilling down into what values are most important to you.

You start with the first two values that are on your list. Then ask yourself any or a combination of the following questions. Sometimes, you may ask one question and the immediate response is not clear. If this happens ask another one of the questions to see what your reaction is.

> *Which of these two values is most important to me right now?*
>
> *If somebody was taking both values away from me right now, which one would I reach out and keep hold of?*
>
> *If I could only wake up and keep one of these two values to live with in the morning which one would it be?*

Having chosen your preferred value out of the two, put the other aside for now and take the preferred value and compare it with the next value down the list. Repeat the same exercise we have just done above and ask the same question(s). For each pair that you compare, there will always be a dominating value that you will move down the list and compare against every one until you have completed a comparison with the very last value. Whichever value you have chosen at the end that you are still holding onto becomes your No. 1 value. Write this down separately as it forms the start of your official hierarchy of values. You now need to identify your No. 2 value. To keep it simple, you now start from the top of the remaining list and repeat the process. Ideally you should apply this process to the whole of the list until you have a complete hierarchy of values.

Following is an example of some of my original values (left hand side). These were in no particular order. On the right is the result as I worked down choosing the most important on the left and writing them in order on the right.

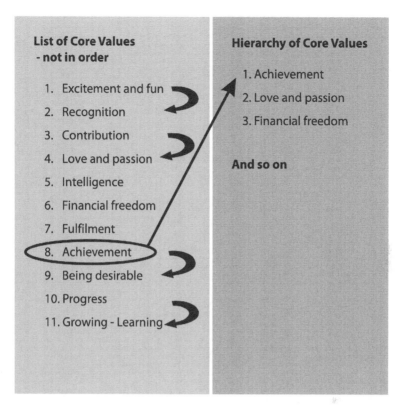

A Self-Assessment

Once you have done this you must congratulate yourself – this was a huge step forward because you are now able to see exactly why you do many of the things you do in life. Looking at the order of your list of values, ask yourself, 'how would a person with these values show up in the world?' How would they act? What would their focus be? Would they be relaxed or stressed? What would their health be like? What would their relationship be like?

This is not about good or bad or right or wrong – these values and their order have defined where you have placed most of your focus, energy and attitude. This should give you a fantastic insight into why you are experiencing many of the emotions in your life right now. Doing this will also help you identify very quickly which values you need to change. That is the next part the exercise.

Creating Your New Hierarchy of Positive Values

Going back to what happened to me – having established what my top values were and the order in which they controlled my life, I became very clear that this was not how I wanted to live my life. I sat down and visualised vividly how I wanted my life to be two years into the future. I asked myself some really powerful questions and through this process I was able to identify what values I would have to live by in order to live such an amazing life. I chose to define this new list of values and then put them in a new hierarchy based on the person I wanted to be in this new life. Let me share with you my revised hierarchy of values.

Rohan's New Hierarchy of Positive Values

1. Health and Vitality
2. Love and Companionship
3. Honesty
4. Intelligence
5. Fun and Happiness
6. Awareness
7. Passion and Enthusiasm
8. Gratitude and Contribution
9. Growth and Knowledge
10. Courage and Determination

Hopefully you can see a dramatic difference in this revised hierarchy of values. For your information, achievement in this revised list came in at number 13. Interestingly, it became really clear to me that no level of achievement would feel fulfilling if I was not healthy, vital, passionately connected with my fiancée and at the same time coming from a place of honesty and fun and happiness. Then, as I sat down and pictured how it would feel to live by these new top values, the truth really hit me. Simply experiencing these values on daily basis would make me feel successful and happy. That alone gave me an immense sense of achievement. That was a powerful awakening for me.

In order for you to establish your new hierarchy of values, you will have to allow yourself a chance to relax and close your eyes. Picture who you really want to be in the future and consider the following questions:

How do you want to experience life?

How do you want to show up in the world?

How would you like to communicate with other people?

How would you like to be in your relationship?

How do you want your health to be?

How would you like to manage your money and create your wealth?

Once you have a clear image of these things, then simply ask the question 'In order to become this person, what Core Values would I need to adopt?' You can use my list and the table of core values above to help give you some guidance. The important thing here is to identify the empowering values that you know will enable you to live as the person you truly want to become.

Having created your own list of empowering values that you want to live by, the next stage is to get them into order of importance. With the list of new values in front of you, it is a simple process of repeating the same exercise as we did previously in choosing between any two values. The key is to work down the list and put them in order of importance as this new person you want to be. Once you have your new primary value, remove it from the main list and it now becomes No.1. You then work down the list to identify No. 2 and so on.

Once you have done the exercise, even just looking at the new list should give you a buzz. Congratulations.

Aligning Your New Values – Become Your Values

I would highly recommend having this list of values written out on a piece of card or on the back of a plain business card to remind you what they are. These values will become your guiding light over the next few months. Constantly remind yourself of which are the top five Core Values. Make sure that you allow them to become part of your everyday actions. Become the values that you have written down. Become happier if happiness is one of your values. Eat healthier if health is one of your top values. Be more loving, intimate and romantic if these are in your top values. In other words, don't just intellectualise this process, become the values you want to experience, live them, act them, feel them and enjoy them.

6 | Step Three
- Change Your Conditions

Welcome To Your Conditions

Having created your own hierarchy of values, the next step in your Change Process is to review the Conditions by which your values have to be satisfied. Basically, for every Core Value that that you have listed you will have a set of Value Conditions that have to be met in order for you to physically be able to experience that particular value. This works exactly the same way a computer program works. It is no different to sitting at a set of road traffic lights. If the light is red (Value Condition) then you don't move forward (Value). If the light is green (Value Condition) then you can move forward (Value). Note that the value in this analogy would be to experience moving forward which is conditional on the colour of the traffic light. If the light never changed from red or only flicked between red and amber, we would never move forward.

Value Conditions play a *huge* role in every decision we make and work in synergy with your values and beliefs. Some Value Conditions help keep you safe; others help you create an amazingly healthy life or a passionate, loyal relationship. Equally, these conditions can also work against us to create such a controlling life that we never experience true excitement and passion.

We *all* have conditions linked to our core values – all of us. However, very few people actually stop to review them and the impact they have on their lives. This is your chance for you to look closely at the Value Conditions you have for every area of your life.

Understanding Your Conditions

Let's take the Core Value of health and fitness which means that feeling healthy and fit is extremely important to you. Imagine I asked you the question, "What conditions have to occur for you to feel healthy and fit?" In response to this question you may say to me that in order to feel healthy and fit one of the conditions that has to be met is that you would have to work out at the gym five times per week. That would represent one of your key value conditions for feeling healthy and fit.

An important step in this process is to now repeat the question. So I would say to you, "Great, what other conditions have to occur for you to feel healthy and fit?" And you might say, *"another condition for feeling healthy is that I need to eat two raw food meals per day."* That becomes a second condition for you to feel healthy and fit. I would then repeat the question again and you might respond with, *"a third condition is that I must not allow my weight to go over 80kg."*

This process should be repeated until you have identified the essential Value Conditions that control the specific Core Value in question. Some Core Values will have more conditions than others.

Exercise – My Primary Value Conditions

Now it is your turn to establish the *condition* that you apply to your Core Values. Taking the top five Core Values that you listed previously, write each core value on the top of a blank page in your journal. Then underneath that title put the following sentence 'The following conditions have to be met for me to .... *insert the value here*'

Core Value: **INTEGRITY**

My Current Value Conditions for feeling INTEGRITY

Any of the following conditions should be met for me to feel that I am acting with INTEGRITY

"I honour my word when I say I will do something for someone"

"I operate in a professional and honest way"

"I focus on people first, not how much I can make out of the deal"

"I don't compromise my values to get a quick solution or to make money"

As shown in the example, write out as many rules that come to mind. Keep repeating the question until you have exhausted the list. It does not matter how many; the important thing is to capture them all. Sometimes it helps to change the question to 'what other conditions would have to occur?' or 'What else would have to happen?'

Please take the time to do the exercise. It may take you an hour or two to work through these top Core Values. You must trust the process here and trust me when I say that this is an invaluable exercise in helping you understand where and why you may be experiencing blocks in your life right now.

How Strict Are Your Conditions?

Some conditions that you have make it very easy to experience a Core Value whilst others make it virtually impossible to achieve the same value. Understanding this is essential to your happiness and success in any area of your life. Value Conditions can be broken into two types – Strict Conditions and Relaxed Conditions.

Strict Conditions

Strict Conditions will always have specific words that suggest that this requirement must happen in order for me to feel, happy, healthy, successful and so on. Therefore, the sentence structure for Strict Conditions will include words or phrases such as *'only if', 'must have', 'have to experience', 'need to'* or *'I will only be able to experience if'.*

In addition to this, Strict Conditions are nearly always linked by the word 'and' in such a way that the value that you are wanting experience can only happen *if* Condition 1 *and* Condition 2 *and* Condition 3 *and* Condition 4 are achieved.

Virtually every person I have worked with who is experiencing a block in their lives or is feeling frustrated has had overly strict value conditions linked with the core values that they wish to experience. You can generally spot somebody who has Strict value conditions in a specific area of their lives because whenever they talk about that subject they appear tense and in many cases highly stressed. Which is not surprising if you think that they are trying to achieve a whole set of conditions which realistically will not be achieved. Let's look at a real example from a client of mine called Bobby.

Bobby's Frustration At Not Feeling Successful In His Life

When I first met Bobby he was in his early 30s working in IT (information technology). Bobby was originally born in India but had been living in the United Kingdom for almost 25 years. He was married with a lovely daughter and had a warm, confident air about him. He kept himself pretty fit and lived what many would consider to be a fairly comfortable lifestyle. So when Bobby came to me it was not clear initially what his challenge in life was.

In his words, having asked him how he thought I could help him, he simply said "Rohan, I just don't feel successful in my life". I used specific questions to get clarity on exactly what he meant by not feeling successful. We then gained clarity on his beliefs and then I coached him through the process for establishing his new hierarchy of values.

What became obvious with Bobby was not an issue with his Core Values. In fact, he had a very strong set of positive Core Values which is why in most areas of his life he was already successful – he had a great family life, he was healthy and enjoyed the experiences with his wife and child. His real frustration came down to *feeling unsuccessful* in his workplace. And the issue was with the Value Conditions that he had applied to being *successful.*

In response to my question, "what conditions have to occur for you to feel successful?" he replied, *"only if my colleagues at work tell me that I have done an excellent job every time I do a piece of work and only when my boss personally acknowledges my results verbally and in a recognition memo to the rest of the department and only if the clients I have worked for ask to work with me again whenever they have a new project and only when at the end of every year I get a pay rise."*

I will stop there, but actually the list was longer!

I think you will be able to see here that Bobby was not feeling successful because it would be virtually impossible for him to experience that unique set of criteria all at the same time consistently. His conditions for success were tying him up in knots. For Bobby to start to feel more successful, that set of very strict conditions had to be relaxed and that is exactly what we did.

One of the main reasons people disagree or fall out in families, relationships, careers and business is because they have different beliefs about the world and also different values or similar values but with very strict rules. Let's say you meet a lady called Mary at a social event. She is very successful in business and you both have lots to talk about as success is one of your Core Values. However, Mary does not value health as highly as you do. She smokes and enjoys drinking alcohol which does not mean she is any lesser person than you, however you may have strict conditions about health that mean that for you to feel healthy, you will not smoke and drink. Now imagine that in addition to that, your Value Conditions for friendship are that you are only friendly with people who do not smoke and they do not drink. In this situation you will probably never develop a friendship with Mary unless you relax your conditions. Although this may sound a little extreme, this type of emotional distancing happens more than people realise because it occurs at a subconscious level. It's not like you walk around with a checklist of conditions. They simply operate in the background, often without you realising.

Exercise – Understanding Your Strict Conditions

A powerful exercise to do is to identify the Core Values in your life where you are currently experiencing some pain, discomfort or frustration. For example, it could be that you want to feel more successful but you are not feeling that way; or maybe you want more excitement in your life but are not getting it. Write the value down and then list out the conditions associated with that specific value as you did before for the other values. Now write out all of these Value Conditions as a paragraph and place the word *and* or *only when* between each of the conditions. Check back with Bobby's example above. If you do this correctly, you will quickly be able to see how strict your rules really are in this area. When placed together like this you get an immediate understanding of why you are finding it hard to feel satisfied in this area of your life. The great thing is that you have the control to relax these rules if you choose.

Relaxed Value Conditions

Relaxing your value conditions is about taking *ownership* over how you want to feel and experience an emotion and a Core Value. Relaxed conditions are much easier to achieve, they are not reliant on other conditions taking place. Most importantly, you must make the conditions linked to *you* allowing them to happen and *not* on some outside influence over which you have no control. For example, if a Core Value is feeling intimacy with your partner, rather than have a condition that relies on your partner such as 'I feel intimate only when my wife kisses me softly when we are relaxing and also gives me a shoulder massage' you can change it so that you have ownership; for example, 'when I take the time to relax with my wife or simply hold her in my arms at the end of the day and kiss her passionately.'

To make your conditions really relaxed you simply need to enable them to be experienced anytime without any other conditions. Plus, when redefining your conditions in a relaxed way you change *and* for *or* so that the rules are not linked.

Mina's Manic Relationship Conditions

I was describing the importance of Value Conditions to Mina, one of my clients recently. Relationship challenges were an issue to her and an area she had asked to work on in our coaching sessions. So I asked her to list the typical conditions she had put on the value of intimacy and the feeling of being loved in a relationship. These are a few of the conditions she wrote:

1. *Call me at least once a day and have the urging need to do so*

2. *Call me straight away when he gets home from work*

3. *Be very tactile every day*

4. *I need to come first above everything else i.e. be willing to drop everything for me*

5. *Anticipate and guess all my needs*

There were a lot more conditions. In all her relationships Mina had been unhappy and in her words, *"First I expect the man I am with to know I feel hurt when he does or doesn't do what I expect him to do. When he breaks my rules, then I will feel the pain, be quiet about it and withdraw in my own world. I will try to avoid acknowledging the pain and protect myself by becoming cold and slightly distant first in my heart and then physically.*

Having written out these conditions Mina actually laughed out loud and the realisation hit her that her conditions were so very strict that there was no way her partners could satisfy all of them at the same time. She began to realise that the issue in the relationships she had previously were with her and not her partners.

Relaxing your Value Conditions is a simple process. Let's take happiness as the Core Value that you want to experience on a regular basis. The new, relaxed condition in this situation could be that you are happy 'anytime you have a loving thought towards your partner' or 'whenever you remember a time that you both laughed and had fun' or 'anytime you send a message to your partner' or 'whenever you send any type of message, email or note to your partner' or 'anytime you think about your first kiss together'.

The essential ingredient here is that the condition is NOT dependent on someone else influencing it. In other words, the condition must be defined as you taking the action or creating the experience. For example, with Mina above she could have said 'anytime I send a message to my boyfriend' rather than 'Only if my partner sends me a text every morning.' Her conditions were all dependent on him rather than her having control of her emotions.

As simple as this process may appear, it is amazingly effective. I have personally experienced the sense of relief that this exercise creates when working on previous conditions that I had which were very strict. I have sat with clients who have broken into tears of happiness as they read back their new conditions and automatically started to feel the shift that takes place by relaxing them – men and women.

Let's see what happened to Bobby from our previous example.

Bobby Changed His Conditions For Feeling Successful At Work

What I loved about Bobby was that he also had a great sense of fun. When he heard me explain about Value Conditions he immediately had a massive awakening. As we looked at his strict conditions for success in his workplace he actually said out loud, "There is no way I would ever achieve this, how crazy is that?"

When I asked Bobby to come up with a new set of conditions for success in his workplace he asked if he could include fun in the process and I said that that would be even better. So here is his new set of conditions for feeling successful in his job. Each of these was separate from the other conditions and the linking word he used was *or* not *and*.

+ *Anytime I complete a piece of work or get a result in anything I am doing*

+ *Whenever I smile at my boss*

+ *Anytime I get a chance to make my colleagues laugh*

+ *Whenever I get to chat with one of my current or potential clients*

+ *Anytime I bounce different ideas off my colleagues*

+ *Anytime I stretch myself*

+ *Anytime I arrange a fun night out for the people in my team*

My New Relaxed Rules Exercise

Taking the top five Core Values that you listed as the ones that you wish to carry forward as the new you, I would like you to rewrite each Core Value on the top of a blank page in your journal. Then, underneath that title, put the following: 'My new relaxed Value Conditions for *(write the core positive value)* are as follows...'

To make these much easier to achieve, you should include terms like 'Whenever I...' or 'Anytime X, Y, Z ...' Once you have written out your relaxed conditions it is really important to have them close to hand as you may wish to check on them regularly for the first 2 to 3 months. The key to the success of this process is to repeat the declarations and remind yourself how well it is working. Only you can be the best judge of how well your new conditions are working. If you are feeling any tension, simply review the conditions and, where necessary, adjust or relax them further. Remember you are reprogramming your own computer so there may be a few bugs to iron out the first few times you run the program.

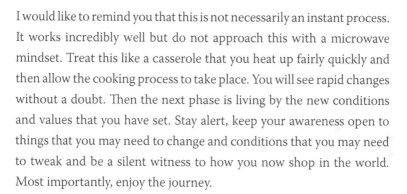

Core Value: **SUCCESSFUL**

Any of the following conditions can be met for me to feel that I am SUCCESSFUL

'Any time I remember all the great things I have achieved already'

'Anytime I think about all the people I have helped'

'Anytime I complete a small or big task'

This Is Not Like a Microwave

I would like to remind you that this is not necessarily an instant process. It works incredibly well but do not approach this with a microwave mindset. Treat this like a casserole that you heat up fairly quickly and then allow the cooking process to take place. You will see rapid changes without a doubt. Then the next phase is living by the new conditions and values that you have set. Stay alert, keep your awareness open to things that you may need to change and conditions that you may need to tweak and be a silent witness to how you now shop in the world. Most importantly, enjoy the journey.

7 | Step Four
- Believe It Or Not, It's True

Introduction

This step in the change process addresses the very foundations of how you make decisions, how you react to the world around you and what drives you forward or stops you in your tracks with fear. We are going to explore your most powerful and influencing beliefs.

Believe it or not, we are not born with any beliefs. We don't arrive and suddenly start believing that we cannot be a doctor, make more money, attract the right partner or climb a certain mountain. These self-defeating beliefs are developed through our lives, and the strongest beliefs are often put in place at an early age. What is scary and at the same time exciting is that there are thousands of these beliefs to choose from and you can choose which ones to adopt at any time in your life.

Like every element of this Six Step Change Process, the investigation of your whole belief system is instrumental in pinpointing what has or is still holding you back in one or more areas of your life. For that very reason, be extra vigilant as we work through this next step of the journey. Notice in particular when you feel resistance to doing an exercise as this may be a critical moment of change occurring. Generally, when we experience a resistance in such a process, it is because we are touching a truth that we know must be addressed and dealt with. That's when you push harder and commit to seeing it through.

The Lady Who Repelled People

On one of the seminars that I was presenting, I spoke with a lady in the audience who had some seriously deep-rooted beliefs about money that had been holding her back for almost a decade. The extent of her fears and negative beliefs about money was so great that people in the audience were trying to avoid her during the coffee breaks. She had an energy around her that appeared to drag people down and she was spreading it like a farmer spreads manure on a field. You may laugh at this comment but the impact on an audience when someone is resonating in such a fearful place can be quite profound.

Imagine for a moment how many people she had influenced with her fear over the last ten years – it could potentially be thousands of people. If someone believes something strongly enough it becomes part of their identity. When that happens, their whole frame of thinking, reasoning and decision-making will be driven by these limiting beliefs.

In the case of the lady in question, what was sad about her situation was that her fears were based on observations linked to her ex-husband and his misuse of their money. Her face was tense when she spoke about money, her shoulders were high and she always shrugged, she stooped and she had almost puppy dog-like eyes when she was talking to anyone about the subject of money. She literally lived the fear through her body and expressions.

The truth is that what she believed did not have to be her reality. However, she made her beliefs and concerns about the future totally real to herself by talking and focusing on them consistently. This crippled her emotionally and physically. She was the victim of a set of *life-sucking* beliefs.

Can a Destructive Belief Spread?

Can a negative belief spread like wildfire? The answer to this question is dependent on three factors:

✦ *How strong the belief is in the person spreading it*

✦ *How believable is it to other people?*

✦ *How insecure the people receiving it are in their own personal beliefs*

Let us take the case of the lady at my seminar. Firstly, after talking with her, I discovered that her ex-husband had taken over £223,000 worth of their equity from their home and put it into projects that he knew nothing about and without really thinking as an investor. He had also chosen partners who had no experience in the area of property and business. When they started to lose money, on the suggestions from these partners, he had continued to draw further funds from the home in order to 'make it better and fix the problem'. They ended losing over £275,000, all of which had come from their home. The divorce followed shortly afterwards.

Put yourself in her shoes for a moment. Be a silent witness and ask yourself, how would you be feeling? What beliefs would you develop around money having gone through this experience? Her major belief issues were around trust of others, trust of herself, fear of money and using money to invest and also anger towards her long-separated husband.

Now you can begin to understand how when I started to talk about using short-term funding to renovate properties the right way and make a profit, this immediately triggered her greatest negative beliefs about money. It was like putting a match to dry open prairie grass with a light wind. I ignited her fear by the very suggestion of using her money for this.

Does any of this sound familiar? Have you ever heard somebody explaining something or possibly had an experience where you have instinctively withdrawn and pulled away because you have a belief that seems to stop you from stepping forward? You resisted a new concept because it challenged you? You avoided getting intimate with someone in a relationship? You avoided investing in something or even in yourself? You avoided taking any risk? If so, right or wrong, it was your beliefs that stopped you taking action.

Make no mistake, beliefs are as real as you *believe* them to be and when consciously managed they can be incredibly empowering. In the examples above, certain beliefs that we hold can actually protect us from making silly, rash decisions. However, if the beliefs are founded on fear and inadequacy, they can equally be incredibly disempowering. What this means is that we have to check in on what we believe about the world and make sure that those beliefs are supporting us in a positive way. If they're not then it's time to kick them into touch, say adios and find more empowering beliefs that will help us achieve our dreams.

It is that simple. It takes work, practice and discipline to shift stubborn beliefs – but it can be done. I have helped thousands of people do it and when accomplished the result is both inspiring to see and highly emotional. From my experience helping people do this in groups and one-on-one, the people that make the biggest shifts are the ones who are open and ready to change and more importantly ready to let go. The seminar environment is powerful; you are totally immersed and emotionally charged and seeing others make changes makes it easier to go there yourself. To do so on your own, you will need to be focused and very disciplined.

Do you believe that it is a habit?

Let's take a quick look at beliefs and how they become so powerfully installed in your psyche and behaviour patterns. Firstly, it is important to realise that a belief is simply a feeling or emotion that you have a great deal of certainty about. That feeling is so strong that you act in accordance with the emotional influence it has over your body. The more often you have this strong feeling (belief), the more embedded it becomes. Therefore, in reality, a recurring belief becomes a habit and you may not even realise it until someone points it out.

As I said earlier we are not born with beliefs which means we must develop them through our lifetime and we do so in the following ways:

- ✦ *Personal experience*
- ✦ *Observations – of parents, brothers, sisters, teachers, work colleagues etc*
- ✦ *Pushed or forced onto us – religion, culture, from generation to generation*
- ✦ *From reading something*
- ✦ *Significant emotional events*

Probably the first people to influence our beliefs at an early age are our parents who do this subconsciously without realising the deep-rooted impact this has on us. At the time of writing this book, my daughter Savannah is nearly two years old. We are currently reading books about child development and one great book we are reading is called *You Are Your Child's First Teacher.* One of the things explained in the book is that more than anything else, children learn by copying what you show them. As you will probably know, mimicking is one of the fastest tools for teaching a child. The same translates to the beliefs that we transfer onto them.

What is profound to me is that every single client that I have worked with on a one-on-one basis or even within a group environment has at least one restrictive, limiting belief that stems from something they learnt from their parents. No matter what age the person is that I'm working with, I know that if I go back far enough in their history, and sometimes it requires going back to the age of two or three, we will find the root cause of one of their current issues. These beliefs become reinforced through repetition. The older you get, the stronger these become until it is simply part of your nature.

Jane's Story – Men Are All The Same

Some years ago I worked with a wonderful lady at a seminar that came to me highly distressed and in tears. Her name was Jane and she was 63 years of age. Jane explained to me that she had never in her adult life had an intimate and lasting relationship with a man. The reason that she was distressed was that she had reached a point in her life where she did not want to spend another year of her life without the opportunity to passionately love a man and to be deeply loved.

She gave me permission to ask her some searching questions and as a result I discovered that she had been sexually abused by a member of her mother's family right up to the age of seven. This experience had left a scar – a set of beliefs about men that she had never been able to heal. Her beliefs were that all men would hurt her, all men were the same deep down and that no man would ever love her for who she was if he knew what had happened to her. This set of beliefs were so deep rooted in her that she had never let a man become close to her in any way and yet she was the most beautiful and radiant woman you could imagine.

Over a period of several hours, deep coaching, visualisation, negative energy release and then extreme negative belief shattering, Jane was able to let go of over 60 years of crippling beliefs. We then created a completely new set of inspiring and passionate beliefs that she wanted to live by for the rest of her life. It was a life-changing process.

Three years later I was speaking at an event and she was in the audience. At the end she came up to me and showed me her left hand. There on her wedding finger was a lovely wedding ring and she wrapped her arms around me and said, "I am a new woman and so in love and he is really cute – thank you so much." I am not sure which one of us cried the most.

You can start to see now how something experienced at an early age with enough reinforcement can have a serious impact on our lives even decades later. Sadly we are not taught in the education that we receive at school how to deal with limiting or destructive beliefs. We simply adopt them and assume that they are right and never question whether we can reprogram ourselves at any time like Jane did at 63 years of age.

As parents we are literally helping to shape a little human being's beliefs. In any situation our children are looking to us to help them create a frame of reference, which then becomes a belief that they adopt and carry forward. For example, some parents condition their affections towards their children based on how well they behave. This can lead to a child developing a belief that in order to receive approval and affection must always look to please others. One impact of this I have observed in some of my clients who later in life struggle in their marriage because they have become pleasers within that relationship and their partner wants someone with more strength and the willingness to challenge and be challenge. All this can stem from a belief installed at an early age.

I would go further here and say that most adults live by a set of beliefs that were formed in their childhood. What this really means is that the majority of people actually live with the belief system of a child. Yes they have been adjusted and reshaped along the way, but some haven't – they have literally been there for decades.

One thing that I would like to say is don't beat yourself up if you have become aware of a belief that has been holding you back. As you can see above, you may not have even been aware of the point in your life where you adopted this belief. However, once it is part of your make up it's just a matter of time and repetition before it becomes a habit. The key is to change the habit.

How Much Do You Really Believe It?

To help you measure the depth of your beliefs I would like to suggest that there are four different degrees of certainty that you associate with beliefs. These degrees of certainty take you from being totally disassociated with the belief to being completely and totally absorbed by it.

Someone Else's Point of View – this is the least influential belief level that you have. This is where you are aware of somebody else's point of view and you may observe it and even discuss it. However, you are not in any way associated with it and do not have a strong opinion either way. These types of beliefs you can choose to take or leave depending on your mood. For example, watching a TV interview with an economist discussing the recession, you understand what she is saying but have no real opinion on the matter.

Your Point Of View – this is the first step to being associated with the belief. It is the lightest level of your personal belief systems where you have a small degree of certainty about what you're saying. However, you are still able to disassociate yourself by sometimes making it someone else's point of view. This level of belief is easily swayed by outside influence. Taking the TV interview above – let's say that you studied economics at school years ago, you may have enough insight and a basic set of beliefs on this subject to agree or disagree with the person being interviewed.

A Personal Belief (*'I believe this to be true'*) – This is simply a feeling that you have with a much greater degree of certainty and conviction. You will have developed your own frame of reference with enough information (experience, observations, passed-on knowledge etc) for you to be convinced that this is true to you. When your belief level is here, you would have to be influenced quite strongly in order to change that belief but it would take considerably more effort than changing your point of view. Back to the TV interview – in this case you like to read magazines and articles online about the recession. Your father did the same and always told you his opinion of how government decisions affect the economy and you have a very similar set of beliefs. Since these are well established and they are different to the lady being interviewed on TV, you find yourself disagreeing with her but her comments have caused you to think about what you believe.

Total Conviction – When you have total conviction, you have a much greater emotional association with the belief. For this reason it is very difficult to change the opinion or belief of somebody who has a very strong conviction. The likelihood is that you will have developed this conviction through external and internal frames of reference and then had it repeatedly reinforced. A final reference to the TV interview as an example – you have studied economics at university, part of your business involves assessing the local economic climate and you have developed some very strong beliefs about why the recession has hit us. You completely disagree with the person on TV and are not swayed by their argument at all.

From my own observations it is the last level of belief above that really empowers and disempowers an individual. If you are reading this book because you have reached a certain point where you simply cannot seem to make progress and you have found the same pattern occurring in the past, the likelihood is that you have a set of beliefs or convictions in this specific area of your life that are holding you back. You must change them or remain in the same place.

Are You Ready To Throw Out The Rubbish?

Releasing your limiting beliefs and replacing them is simply down to applying a process. It certainly helps to work with an experienced coach or mentor, since they can press certain buttons and push you when you need to be pushed. However, you can start right now by releasing your most crippling beliefs and creating a whole new chapter in your life.

Imagine you are standing in the basket of a hot-air balloon. This massive canopy of hot air above you is trying to lift off the ground. You have a lever that you can pull which releases hot air into the balloon giving you more lift. However, there are also large cloth bags full of rocks hanging over the edge of the basket that are so heavy they are restricting your lift-off. The only way to really get the balloon off the ground quickly is to release all of the baggage which will make the basket much lighter and adding more hot air to the balloon to create more lift. This is a simple metaphor to help you understand that the hot-air represents your new, empowering beliefs and bags of ballast represent the negative, restrictive beliefs that you have been carrying most of your life.

In simple words: *dump the garbage and put some good stuff back in.*

It DOES NOT work if you start letting go of the negative stuff and forget to put strong, positive beliefs in place. In fact, what I have witnessed in the past is when a person goes through the releasing process, if they do not immediately replace the old beliefs with new positive beliefs, they nearly always start to fill the void with new negative beliefs.

So let us get ready for lift off. For each area of your life that you want to work on allow an hour or so to really go through this process. There are five stages for letting go of destructive beliefs and replacing them with powerful, constructive beliefs.

Stage 1: *Name and shame the destructive beliefs*

Stage 2: *Be clear on what they have cost you*

Stage 3: *Destroy them*

Stage 4: *Replace the old beliefs with new empowering beliefs*

Stage 5: *Celebrate*

So let's get started. My suggestion is that you first read through this process so that you understand what is needed. You will need a few tools to hand like a pen, loose paper, matches or lighter.

Stage 1: *Name and shame the destructive beliefs*

Let us agree that any negative or restrictive belief that you currently hold in any area of your life is completely and utterly detrimental to your personal growth and wealth. To simplify this further, take a few pieces of paper in front of you. At the top of the paper write 'Negative or limiting beliefs' and in brackets next to this the word 'Garbage'. This is exactly how I want you to see the limiting beliefs, they represent rubbish or garbage that has been hanging around your mind, clogging up your flow and holding you back. When I am working one-on-one with a client, I ask for permission to use direct and powerful language to ensure that we really get impact behind the process. If they say yes, then I say to them, the reality is that these are negative **B**elief **S**ystems, and when you take the initials, B/S, what does that stand for? They usually smile and respond with, "These really are B/S". Remember, these beliefs have not served you, they have held you back and they have sucked away some of your life. They are B/S.

Let us stay with the 'garbage' list to start with. To make this effective you need to focus in on the one area in your life that you wish to improve, to unblock or to change. Pick one now e.g. health, relationship, career, financial or you can be even more specific.

Staying focused on only the one area for now, I want you to write several leading sentences in your journal but do not complete them at this stage. I would recommend making each sentence the title with, say, half a page after one where you are going to write your own response. Let me give you a few examples.

Money

   ✦ *The reason I have so little money in my bank account is because...*

   ✦ *The reason I am in debt is because...*

   ✦ *The reason I am not financially independent is because...*

Relationships

✦ *The reason my relationship feels so unfulfilling and bad is because...*

✦ *The reason we are not intimate and have drifted apart is because...*

✦ *The reason I can't seem to find the right partner is because...*

Career & Business

✦ *The reason I have not changed jobs yet is because...*

✦ *The reason I have not asked for a pay rise is because...*

✦ *The reason I have not expanded my business is because...*

✦ *The reason I have not started a business is because...*

Once you have created at least three leading questions in the area you wish to focus on, you can then start the process of answering the questions.

You must be persistent in this process. Ask the same question over and over again before moving to another question. Each time you ask the question, write down a different response. Then ask the question again and write down a different response. Keep going until you truly believe you have exhausted the list. Do not hold back and do not intellectualise this process. Speak from the heart and capture everything that flows through you.

When I am running a seminar, I will often ask my audience to finish this sentence, 'The reason I have not truly achieved many of my big goals is because...' or 'The reason I am not truly living the life I wanted to be living by this time in my life is because...' The following responses are actual answers that have come from audience and clients around the world:

✦ *I don't have enough money*

✦ *I don't have the right education*

+ *I'm too old*
+ *I'm too young*
+ *I don't have the energy*
+ *I'm too busy and don't have enough time*
+ *It's not good to earn more than you need*
+ *I have to be wealthy to be able to make more money*
+ *I don't have the right look*
+ *I'm too short*
+ *My teacher told me I am not smart enough*
+ *I was told I cannot do it because I am an engineer*
+ *I can't do it because my wife won't let me*
+ *I can't do it because my husband won't let me*
+ *I can't find opportunities*
+ *I've never been very good at meeting the right person*

Some of these are *Other People's Point of View*, others are *Personal Beliefs* and others are strong *Convictions*. If you could imagine yourself carrying just a few of these beliefs around with you, I'm sure you agree that when an opportunity to do or be something different comes along, it is highly likely that you would not take it because of your strength of conviction in one or more of these beliefs.

Worse still, what people often do is they will look for other beliefs that strengthen the main negative underlying belief. They will filter out using their reticular formation in the brain, so that all they see are other negatively supporting beliefs. This leads to an even stronger belief that they cannot try something different or be someone different. The belief then becomes self-fulfilling.

Stage 2: *Be clear on what these beliefs have cost you*

No matter what anybody else tells you, in your heart, deep down in your soul you will know exactly how much a negative limiting belief has cost you. I'm not just talking about financial cost. What I'm talking about here is the cost of having your life sucked out of you; the cost of opportunities that you have missed; the cost of passionate moments that have been lost because your beliefs have stopped you from taking action; the cost to your health and vitality; the cost of time freedom simply because you did not act in the past; the opportunity that you may have had to help another human being or thousands of other human beings. And yes, without doubt there are financial costs to having limiting beliefs.

So let's not beat around the bush, there are certain things that you have not achieved yet in your life and these have been stopped by a set of beliefs that have stopped you getting to where you truly want to get to in your life right now.

The same way alcoholics who attend Alcoholics Anonymous must first acknowledge the fact that they are alcoholics, the first step to negative belief busting is to acknowledge that you have negative beliefs. For many men, pride stops them acknowledging this. Imagine that, something as simple as pride could stop a man from becoming financially independent, from finding a soul mate or from spending more time with his kids.

So let's be humble and acknowledge that every single one of us has beliefs that potentially hold us back in one or more areas of our lives. Me included. Imagine how much more exciting your life could be if you could simply redefine what you believe about the world. Imagine also that part of this process is growth and expansion, so that you could identify at any time the limiting beliefs in different parts of your life that are holding you back. Imagine being able to destroy them at any time. How exciting would that process be?

One powerful approach to busting old negative beliefs is to associate a massive amount of pain with each specific belief and then to completely destroy them physically and emotionally. There are several different ways to do this, but I would like to share the one that I have found most effective for myself and the many clients I have worked with which involves nine steps:

1. Find a place where you can close your eyes, take a deep breath and relax for 10 minutes.

2. As you breathe, allow your body to settle calmly into your chair and start to picture your life at the moment with your existing negative belief or beliefs that are holding you back.

3. Think about the tension and the sick feeling it can create in your body every time you experience this belief. Don't hold back – live it!

4. Think about how much it costs you to hold onto these beliefs. What negative impact has it had on your bank account, your time, health, relationships and family so far?

5. As you are visualising, increase the size of the image in your mind, make it more colourful, imagine turning up the sound and magnify the internal sensations that your body experiences as a result of these negative beliefs. Become aware of how physically draining it is to constantly hold onto these beliefs. In your darkest hours, what pain have these beliefs cost you?

6. Now start to look into the future and imagine the impact these beliefs will have on your life in the future. What are the worst possible things that could happen by holding on to these ridiculous and disempowering beliefs? What will you miss out on? What dreams will disappear? How will your health be affected? What will it do to your family and love life? How will it affect your financial situation?

7. Look out into the future two, five, ten years and more. Picture the worst.

8. When you get to a point where you can really feel the impact of these negative beliefs and how they will negatively impact your life, say to yourself, "That is enough". Remind yourself that you never, ever want this to become reality. Say to yourself that you will do whatever it takes to destroy these limiting beliefs now in order to achieve your desires.

9. You have a choice here to either open your eyes for the next stage or carry out the closed eye process in stage three.

If I was working with you one-on-one I would give you greater leverage and ask you to imagine you were talking to your children or closest family members and ask you to look them in the eye and tell them what this has cost you and them. Explain to them why you are not prepared to live with these ridiculous beliefs any more. This creates massive emotional leverage.

Stage 3: *Throw the garbage out and destroy the old stuff*

Whilst in this emotional place of clarity, eyes closed and totally committed, I would like you to use one of two approaches, the first requires you to stay in this place with your eyes closed and the second requires you to open your eyes and take physical action. If you choose to, you could go through approach one and then do approach two, the choice is yours.

Approach 1

Holding on to the conviction that you will do whatever it takes to destroy these limiting beliefs, I want you to take a deep breath and at the same time imagine your list of all your negative beliefs evaporating into nothing – ONE BY ONE see them disappear. If you want to be more aggressive about this you can imagine the list being burnt or blown up by an explosion. The key is to use whatever visual and emotional experience works for you in order to destroy the belief in your mind. Picture taking out a hammer and smashing them up, liquidise them, fire them into space – basically destroy them.

Approach 2

Open your eyes and grab your original list of negative beliefs that you have written down. Grab a box of matches and screw up the paper into a ball. Go outside, or if you are near a fireplace use that. Holding the paper in your strongest hand, look at it and repeat out loud to yourself why you want to destroy this B/S. State clearly why you are not prepared to live with this anymore. Take a deep breath and put the paper down and light the match. Then set fire to the paper and watch every part of it burn – completely.

Every man and woman that I have worked with that has truly embodied this process has gone through massive changes in this process. Some cry, others breathe a huge sigh of relief – but the reality is that it works if you allow it too.

Natalie's First Step to Letting Go

My business partner Raj Deb and I have a CD Program called *The Millionaire Factor 'Your Journey Begins'*. Included in this CD Program is a section where we explain the part of the process of Belief Busting.

Natalie is an attendee from one of my seminars who, having recently listened to our CD Program, emailed after working through part of the above process. What a lovely outcome.

I am writing to you both today because you are so inspirational and I would love to say a really HUGE THANK YOU and to share my inner thoughts with you both.

I purchased a copy of your audio CD'S 'THE Millionaire Factor' several weeks ago and I have just had the most amazing experience on exercise No1 'burning' my fears & beliefs.

On your sound advice I went and purchased a really special journal and my journey began. It took me days to write them all down, all very heart wrenching and there was a lot of tears, I got there in the end.

I put on my best outfit and really dressed up for the occasion. I lit the BBQ and had someone filming me (I love filming really special occasions and I did it.) I watched them burn into smoke one by one - yelling at the top of my voice 'they are all' BUL-S- - IT, I DO NOT NEED THESE FEARS' seeing each one dissolve made me feel a complete release was happening.

I would like to share with you that there have been occasions when I have stood with clients as they have held the crumpled list in their hand. At the point where I asked them to put the paper down in the fireplace and light it with a match they have actually frozen. They cannot let go of the paper. Usually, I need to step in and coach them a little bit to remind them of the intense pain it will cause if they don't let go now.

The reason they do not want to release the paper is because they are being asked to burn a part of who they are. Many of these beliefs make up their whole identity. Imagine being asked to have a part of your identity removed. The natural reaction is to freeze because the immediate emotional question is, 'what do I do now, what do I believe now, who am I now if I let go of this?' All of these things go through your mind in an instant.

For this very reason, once you have released all the garbage and destroyed it you must move rapidly to Stage 4.

Stage 4: *Start your own Belief Adoption Agency*

This is the stage where you get to rewrite your personal life book, where you define what you want to believe and how those new beliefs will mould your life in the future.

I would like you to think of yourself as an adoption agency for empowering beliefs. Imagine that you could look out at the world and study some of the most amazing human beings that have existed and still exist on this earth. And from this study, you could identify the most empowering beliefs that these great individuals hold. Now in your journal write down the heading 'Inspiring People' and then beneath that write the names of the people who most inspire and motivate you.

Then underneath this list of names, put the title 'Their Inspiring Beliefs.' Beneath here, list out as many positive beliefs that you believe they have or have developed in order to become who they are. Have some fun with this. Walk around as though you were that person, stand, talk, look at yourself as though you were one of these inspiring people. As you become inspired, capture on paper each and every belief. To help you, ask yourself 'If I was this person, what would I believe about this area of life?' 'What would I believe about money?', 'What would I do to make my relationship more passionate?', 'What would I believe about success and taking chances?' Let it flow.

To help you in the process of finding and adopting new empowering beliefs I have summarised a small study of six very different people who I believe have achieved success in their chosen profession or life purpose. Some of them you may be familiar with whilst others you may not. For each of these people, I have selected one belief that I think is characteristic of their personality and success. This will provide you with at least six empowering beliefs that you may or may not choose to adopt for yourself.

Evander Holyfield

(three times boxing heavyweight champion of the world)

Evander Holyfield was underestimated from an early age by many of the adults who coached him. In 1984 he became recognised in the boxing world when he was unfairly disqualified in the Olympics three rounds short of a gold medal. Through pure persistence he went on to become the heavyweight champion of the world. He was later defeated and lost his title and then through sheer determination and passion regained it. Never afraid to take on anybody who challenged him, he continued to defend his title. Then, due to a heart condition, Evander was forced to retire from boxing. Amazingly, with the passion of boxing still within, he decided to return to boxing and successfully gained the title for a third time.

> *Belief:* Evander Holyfield believes that his defeats and setbacks were simply stepping stones to enable him to grow and become an even greater and more skilful boxer.

Tom Basso *(stock market futures trader)*

I learned about Tom Basso when first reading a book called *New Market Wizards* by Jack Schwager. I have included him here because I really loved the way Jack Schwager summarised Tom Basso and how he had measured his success. Basso is not regarded as a legendary trader. However, he has averaged a return of 20% annually since 1987 as a stock market accounts manager handling considerably large sums of money. His minimum account size to my knowledge is $1 million per client. What impressed me from Schwager's description was the calm and relaxed manner in which he conducts his trading operations. In a market that is incredibly volatile, his approach, his systems and his methodology has yielded consistent results year after year. Anybody reading this book who is interested in trading would do well to study the approach that he uses. In an industry where people die of heart attacks through stress, Basso's performance is outstanding.

> *Belief:* Tom Basso believes in focusing his total attention on trading well and that the results will take care of themselves. And while focusing his attention on his trading, he also believes that if you keep your emotions in balance, rather than allowing them to fluctuate up and down which creates exhaustion, then trading can become fun.

Goldie Hawn *(Academy award-winning Actress and Mother)*

Whether you are male or female I would strongly recommend you read more about this amazing lady; in particular her book called *A Lotus Grows In The Mud*. For much of her early life Goldie Hawn was not particularly happy with her looks. In her own words, her eyes were too big, her nose was too flat, her ears would stick out, her mouth was too big and her face was too small. She even had a challenge with her name Goldie. Her career did not take off immediately like some actors; it took work and several personal and professional set-backs. Despite these set-backs and early negative beliefs about her appearance Goldie Hawn went on to become an incredibly successful actress and a household name. Her marriage to Kurt Russell the actor has been one of the most successful marriages in Hollywood and her daughter, Kate Hudson, has pursued an equally successful path under the guidance and love from her mother. She is an incredibly insightful woman who is not afraid to voice her opinion about life. She is openly candid about both the good and bad experiences that she has had on her journey as a woman, an actress, a mother and wife.

> **Belief:** Goldie believes that we are always going to make choices in our life, some of which turn out badly. However, she believes we should not dwell on them and that they provide us with the ability to learn from our mistakes and remind us not to go that way again. She believes that change is inevitable, that we should not dwell on our mistakes and that we must adapt in order to evolve as human beings.

Frank Dick O.B.E

(a former director of coaching for British athletics)

I was privileged enough to watch Frank Dick speak many years ago at a seminar and I was truly inspired by his philosophy on the power of teams. Frank Dick became the director of coaching for British athletics at a time when the eastern bloc countries had been dominating athletics for some 25 years. In August of 1989, under the powerful coaching and guidance of Frank Dick, the British men's athletic team took the European Cup for the first time. On 5th August during that event, with the team lagging on the score board, these are the historic words that he said to the team that changed everything: *"You guys go through life as individuals in an individual sport, but over the next two days you'll each need each other to achieve. You have a 14-point mountain to climb: that's the difference between what you are worth on paper and what the opposition is worth. If you are worth one point and can turn it into two, it gives us just as big a foot up the mountain as if you are worth seven and can turn it into eight points. Remember what your task is here today: one point more than you are worth."* Since then Frank Dick has become a prolific coach to some of the greatest athletes in the world including people like Boris Becker and Mary Joe Fernandez.

> **Belief:** Frank Dick believes wholeheartedly that overall success in any endeavour, especially sport and business, is a result of the team we have around us; and that unbelievable odds can be overcome by trusting the team we work with.

Tony Barley RIP *(Engineer & Businessman)*

Tony Barley, or 'The Anchor Man' as he became affectionately known to those in the field of Geotechnical and Civil Engineering, was a long-standing friend, past business partner and one of my first mentors in my life as a Civil and Geotechnical Engineer. When I was working on my PhD in the late 1980s and early 1990s, Tony Barley's experience and knowledge, together with that of my PhD Supervisor, Professor Stuart Littlejohn, were essential to my success. Not satisfied with what conventional engineering practice offered to provide slope support for road cuttings and deep excavations, Tony went on a mission starting in the 1970s to develop new systems of support. This passion led to the patenting of a new system called the SBMA which he continued to develop through the 80s, 90s and into the 2000s. What makes this story more uplifting is that during this time, Tony discovered that he had an unusual condition resulting in an expanding heart. Month by month, this became progressively more and more life threatening.

Like most new concepts, especially in the conservative world of civil engineering, the idea was slow to be picked up by the industry, and criticised by some engineers. But like all great success stories, Tony refused to be perturbed and for 30 years he persisted with showing people his system. Now in 2010, this system is being used all over the world. Sadly Tony passed away in August of 2009 but his legacy, passion and vision still live through those that knew and loved him. I was one those people and he is dearly missed.

> **Belief:** Tony Barley believed that when you have an idea that you are passionate about that can benefit your industry and the world, then you must continue to pursue that dream and to share the message with everyone who will listen – and even those that don't

want to listen. He believed that if something does not work then there will always be another way to solve the problem.

Lynn Twist *(Global Activist and Fund Raiser)*

Lynn Twist is someone I have already mentioned in this book; she is one of the world's truly inspirational people. Her passion for fundraising spans decades and globally she has raised well in excess of $150 million in individual – not corporate or government – but individual contributions for charitable causes. She has worked in this field for over 40 years and met and worked with some of the wealthiest and poorest people on the planet, including Mother Theresa. For half of her career, Lynn Twist worked with The Hunger Project, an organisation dedicated to ending world hunger. She has worked with all cultures of the world, both modern and 'ancient'. Through these amazing experiences she has developed an incredible insight into money and how people perceive it, relate to it and live with it. From the poorest to the richest, she has observed patterns that show up again and again. She continues to not only raise millions of dollars in contributions, but also to raise the global consciousness about money, how to deal with it and how to use it for greater causes.

> *Belief:* Lynn Twist believes that we can all develop a different and healthier relationship with money such that we can use it for a higher cause. In her book *The Soul of Money* she states that "The soul of money offers a way to realign our relationship with money to be more truthful… enabling us to live a life of integrity and full self-expression that is consistent with our deepest core values, no matter what our financial circumstances."

Other beliefs you may want to consider include:

✦ *I am ready and open to receiving more money into my life*

✦ *I deserve to be successful in my career*

✦ *I am a passionate and loving husband/wife*

✦ *Opportunities flow in my direction every day*

✦ *I can achieve anything I put my mind to*

✦ *If I don't know how to do something, I always find someone who does*

✦ *I get healthier every day by eating quality food and doing simple exercise*

So once you have established your overall list of empowering beliefs, choose the ones that YOU would really like to adopt. Now the process is simple:

1. Start picturing the positive, empowering beliefs that you want to adopt. These must be strong beliefs that you know align with who you are and that will help you to achieve your goals and make positive improvements in the area you are currently focusing on. See them clear and bold. State them out loud if you wish. Go over the list of beliefs and repeat them again and again.

2. In your mind look out into the future and picture living with these new beliefs. Allow yourself to see, feel and hear how these new beliefs will change your life for the better. Run the images like a movie. Become the new you with the new beliefs and feel a new surge of energy flow through you. Smile, laugh and allow yourself to feel totally happy with the new beliefs and changes that have taken place. Fast-forward the images back and forth with you clearly right in the middle of the picture. Exaggerate these amazing beliefs and allow them to completely become who you are. Repeat faster and faster, again and again.

3. As you feel these great emotions and the positive changes, repeat your beliefs to yourself as you slowly open your eyes feeling great.

4. Now write down the new beliefs again in words that are yours and in the present. 'I am an amazing communicator', 'I am the ultimate loving and romantic partner', 'I am a money magnet and attract opportunities every day' or if you have lost someone, 'My family love me and my son is with me everywhere I go in spirit'.

5. Make them part of your daily life.

Stage 5: *Celebrate and be Grateful*

The most important thing that you can and must do is to celebrate and express gratitude for your success. Only a tiny fraction of the percentage of the population ever comes close to doing an exercise like the one you have just done. You have genuinely taken a massive step forward. Go out for a meal, catch a movie, go and party, dance, make love, do something positive to reinforce what you have just done.

Gratitude and celebration have been proven through research around the world to create a powerful chemical benefit to the body. We feel better about ourselves. We feel calmer. We reward ourselves for things that we have done well and do it without guilt and it feels great. Unconditional gratitude is one of the most powerful forces in the universe. Try it. Allow it to be part of this process. Simply reach out and say "thank you."

A Quick Summary

The key with all these things is follow-through. In that respect, I recommend that you track your progress, the positive changes that take place and any tweaks that you need to make. Don't relax and slip into apathy, which can happen. Keep your finger on the button and keep the heat up.

1. Implement and practice each belief.

2. Become aware of their power in your life and observe the response each new belief makes to you.

3. Reinforce to yourself through repetition how positively each new belief is helping shape your life and the decisions you make. Be grateful.

4. Notice how much clearer you feel and decisive you become.

5. Keep a journal for a few weeks to record your emotions and the changes that have taken place.

6. Keep this process up until you find that the new beliefs have become a habit.

If you find the old belief creeping in, then stop, observe the shift in your body, remind yourself how bad this belief is for your life and why you don't even want to entertain it. Go quickly into your mind and pull up the image of your life how it was with this old destructive belief and how bad it will get if you decide to go back to the old beliefs.

It will take some discipline, but keep at it. Remember that some of your habits will have been 'installed' years ago and had years of reinforcement. So when you apply the new ones keep congratulating yourself and reinforce positive statements to strengthen the new behaviour and crush the old.

So that is the process. Is it that simple? Well, yes and no. The key here is to repeat the process if you need to and apply more pain to the old beliefs and pleasure to the new ones. Most importantly be persistent with changing your old limiting beliefs. If you do this you will start to notice positive changes in your thoughts, actions and how you act with other people and how they start to treat you.

8 | Step Five - Create A Supportive Environment

Understanding Your Environments

This part of the Change Process is one that can easily be overlooked and yet is so important to enhancing and sustaining the changes that you have made. We are going to explore the importance of controlling the environments that affect your inner and outer world. So far throughout this book the primary focus has been to work on your inner environment or your inner world. Some of the areas that we have discussed such as changing your beliefs, the language that you use when you are talking to yourself and the conditions that you apply to your values are all inner-world related.

There is, however, an equally important environment that affects how you live your life which we will call your external environment. This external world can also impact you at many different levels. In some cases your external world can literally drag you down or lift you up depending on how you react to those external circumstances. Sometimes you can choose your external environment and on other occasions you have no choice.

The underlying message of this chapter is to understand the importance of your inner and outer world and, where necessary, look at how to change them.

It Starts on the Inside

It has been my belief for many years that irrespective of what is happening in our external environment, one thing that we can control is how we react and the perception that we place on these external circumstances. I have said this in different ways throughout the book. Put another way, you can choose what you think and feel at any one time.

I realize this may sound simplistic. In fact, you might respond by saying that surely there are times when a person is experiencing extreme grief or shock and under those circumstances they cannot control how they think and feel. When something extreme occurs this is true, our body is designed to protect us first remember. However, I believe that once we have experienced our grief, if we have the right resources and people to support us, we can start to change our perception of our current situation so that we start to feel better and therefore slowly move forward in our life.

To help better understand this, I would like to share with you a very personal experience.

My Father's Death – My Mother's Strength

My father had his first stroke at 27 years of age. By the time he met mother he was on experimental drugs and when they married they had given him about 10 years to live. I can still remember that day my father died – he was approximately the same age that I am today as I write this book. That was 31 years ago and I was 13 years of age. I recall that there were a lot of phone calls coming into the house. There seemed to be a lot happening that morning in a flurry. There were several other external influences happening: family calling, my aunties and uncles wanting to speak with my mother, to me and my brothers and even neighbours knocking on the door. My mother must have been feeling an immense mixture of emotions all at once and on top of that, she was now a single mother, with three young boys whom she was responsible for.

It would have been very easy, having nursed my father through a decade of heart and stroke-related illnesses for my mother to feel overwhelmed at that point. Instead, in her darkest hour, my mother chose to control her internal world by focusing on my two younger brothers and me. She did not allow the massive influence of the loss of my father and all the other things around to leave her helpless and overwhelmed. I can still recall how resourceful she became during that time whilst giving us the chance to understand what had happened.

My mother took control of what she knew she could control – her inner world; irrespective of how bad things seemed in the outer world or how much grief and pain she was in, she knew she had to focus on us. In doing so she helped three young boys through what was an emotionally tough time for each of us.

The important thing to take from this story is that in moments of extreme challenge or pain, we still have the ability to change our mental environment and how we react to the outside world. We still need to have time to reflect, experience the pain and the loss at some point and in some cases that is exactly what we need to do. Grief and mourning are a part of coming to terms with the loss of a loved one. And then there will be a time when we know we need to move on.

Ultimately, whether it is a business that has failed, money that you are struggling to manage, a relationship that is not working, your health that is not where you want it to be or the loss of a loved one, you and I have no option but to move forward with our lives. It does not serve us to allow our inner environment to remain negative and in pain. We have to change our perspective, give the experience a different meaning, change our beliefs and create a more inspiring vision of the future.

> **Remember** – from everything that we have discussed so far we know that what we believe and feel on the inside is translated to how we act and behave and articulate on the outside. Therefore, the quality of your life is a direct reflection of how you control your internal environment.

An Internal Environmental Check

I would like you to think of your inner world like the inside of your home or the place where you currently live. You can look out of the windows and see the garden, the surrounding environment and everything beyond the walls of your house. What you are looking at there is the outer world that we have just been discussing. As you turn around and look back inside your home what you are looking at is your inner world. Consider the following questions as you look around your home:

How messy does your house look?

How cluttered is it?

Are there things lying around that have been there for a long time?

Do you have unnecessary newspapers and magazines that can be cleared away?

Does the inside of your home need redecorating?

Does your home have a warm feeling or a cold feeling?

Are there pictures of family and people that you care about?

The image of the inside of your home is a metaphor for the inside of your mind. This internal environment is where you live every single day. The big question to ask as you look around your home (your mind) is 'do I feel comfortable living in this place every day?'

You have probably heard of Feng Shui which is an ancient Chinese art and science that originates back over 2500 years. Feng Shui is a philosophy around the flow and balance of universal energy within any environment. Actually, its early use was around the orientation of monuments and tombs of spiritual significance. Feng Shui literally means wind and water, and works on the belief that if you place and orientate 'possessions' and buildings in a specific way you will attract greater health, wealth and good fortune. The flow of water and wind will be in harmony.

This is exactly what you must do with your Inner Environment – you must exercise some mental and emotional Feng Shui. In order to do that you simply need to work on four areas.

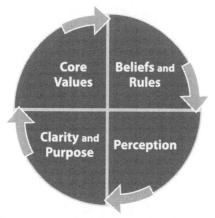

In previous chapters we discussed in detail your beliefs, Value Conditions, Core Values and shifting your perception. Clarity and purpose help give you direction and alignment as will each of the three other elements the same way Feng Shui helps align the energies in your home.

Clarity and Purpose

I believe it is virtually impossible for you to truly define your beliefs, Value Conditions and Core Values relating to your life if you do not have clarity about who you want to be and about the purpose for how you wish to live your life. This may sound profound and I find that some people ignore this area of their life simply because 'they do not know what they want or what their purpose is.' The problem with this belief is that lack of purpose and clarity leads to lack of direction, which leads to lack of results, which in turn leads to frustration and it is usually at this point that you start to feel like you are not moving forward. Which is when you start to go out looking for a solution!

John's Dilemma: Should I Sell My Business?

I worked with a wonderful client, John, who had built a very successful manufacturing business making hand-made furniture for clients. John truly loved the shaping of an idea into a final product that his clients could have in their homes. He had been doing this for almost 15 years. When I met John, however, although he had experienced financial success, he was also bored. He was a decisive, successful businessman who was bored with working in the business. He had two young children and was married to Ruth who loved him very much and who also ran a successful business from home. What emerged from our first session was that over the years of building his business, John had not spent as much time with his family as he had truly wanted to.

I asked John how I could help him. He was already successful in what he was doing. He said, "Rohan, I am bored doing what I am doing in the business and I don't want to let my employees and customers down and I can't decide what to do. I would love for the business to remain a success but there is nobody in the company who can do the job as well as I can. Should I sell my business or close it down?"

This last statement is the classic downfall of many small businesses – the belief that nobody can do the job better than me. John, however, had sustained his success by putting in the hours and total commitment and keeping the business at a certain level.

I told him that the solution was simple – he needed clarity. So I asked him what would be his dream situation in two years' time. "If anything was possible, paint me a clear and vivid picture."

He did exactly that, and it was really obvious that he genuinely wanted to maintain the success of the business, the brand and his loyal staff to keep their jobs. His goal then shifted to only working one day per week in the business and that he would find a person who could take an equity share in the business and run it for him. His purpose was to spend more time with his family and pursue his personal passions, one of which was sailing.

The clearer and more specific we got with this image, the easier his decision-making process was. John had the answer already inside him; he simply needed clarity of vision and strong purpose.

An External Environmental Check

As we have already discussed, your ultimate goal is to develop the ability to control your inner environment. However, if you are constantly bombarded by external influences that chip away at your inner world, even the process of maintaining a positive outlook can be draining. What this means is that you must also be aware of what external influences there are around you at any one time. In some situations you have no choice but to deal with what is happening around you. In other situations you have the ability to choose whether to stay in that environment or to leave it.

I would like to focus on what environments can influence you and also what actions you can take to change those environments. Let us zoom in on your external world and make a note of the different elements that it comprises.

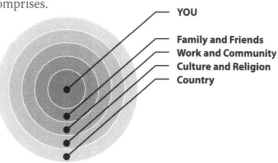

YOU
Family and Friends
Work and Community
Culture and Religion
Country

Family & Friends

Each of these different external environments has a greater or lesser degree of influence on your inner world. More specifically these environments can have a very powerful impact on your beliefs and your perception of the world. You can see from the diagram that the immediate sphere of influence is your family and close friends. From an early age you may not even be aware of the impact these people are having on your life.

This can be a difficult area to address especially when it comes to family. I know for a fact I am very different to my brothers. We each have our own personalities and live our lives with different beliefs and rules and the same thing applies to my mum. In many families people become frustrated because they do not always see eye to eye. Children grow into adults and they evolve certain beliefs that are very similar to their parents' and other beliefs that are completely different. This can be a cause of conflict in the family environment.

Equally when it comes to friends, some of the people that you may associate with may have views about the world that are different to yours. In some cases, when you were younger, your views and theirs were very similar and now as an adult your view of the world is different. This is one of the reasons people drift apart as they get older.

Can these differences cause conflict? Absolutely. At the same time there will be specific values and beliefs that you have that are in complete alignment with those of family members and friends. If an immediate family surrounds you who are supportive of your beliefs then that is a fantastic situation and you should nurture this. For example, you may have the desire to completely change career or start your own business because two of your Core Values are variety and independence. If your family have similar values and beliefs, then they will support your decision and encourage you through the process even during the more challenging times.

On the other hand, if you do not feel that your family and friends are providing you with the support you need or that they do not align with your beliefs and values then you may need to consider the amount of time you should be spending in these relationships. That is a tough thing to think about when it comes to family.

In order to help you make this decision, there are certain questions that you can ask yourself when it comes to friends, family and associates. I would like to give you a few questions to consider and remember that the objective here is to make no judgments. I would like you to be a silent witness and to consider the answer to each question. You may wish to write these in your journal.

Are they positively or negatively focused with their words?

Do they talk about other people and things or about what they are passionate about?

Do they focus a lot on what they hear and see in the media?

Are they abundant in their nature?

Do they talk about themselves and their story a lot?

Do they ask you about your life and what exciting things you are doing?

Do their beliefs, rules and values support or conflict with yours?

Do they generally blame others or take responsibility?

Are they focused on the present and future or linger more in the past?

Do you feel uplifted, indifferent or drained by them?

Hopefully you are starting to get an idea of the energy and emotional state that other people can give off when they are around you. If your conclusion is that the people around you are not helping you to move forward then you must decide how much contact you want to have with them on a regular basis. And yes this can be a very difficult position when it comes to family. This is not a question of love. We are still able to love our family and close friends whilst choosing to restrict the type of conversations that we have with them. This is the first level of controlling your external environment.

We Love Our Family – But It's Time To Move

I have two friends, Amanda and Robert who were attendees to a property seminar I taught in 2004. After the seminar they discovered quickly that their parents were not supportive of the decision they had made to invest £15,000 into their wealth education and develop a property business. Both of them have got great energy, they are passionate, open to learning and love helping people. Robert's home is originally Australia and Amanda's family are UK based. At the time they both lived close to her family in the UK.

As much as they loved Amanda's family, they both realized that staying close to non-supportive friends and family was going to hold them back from achieving their dream of financial independence. They identified an area of the country that they wanted to invest in and they made the decision to move away from the family. To be specific, they moved over 3-hours' drive away! It was a difficult decision to make, but both felt it would be best for their relationship and their family.

The lovely end to this story is that Amanda and Robert achieved their goal of financial independence a few years after moving and her parents eventually moved up north to join them a little later. Now the family are a lot more open and positive about what they do. When I last spoke with them both they had plans in place to move back to Robert's home country, Australia, and they were able to do so living off the monthly rental income from their UK property portfolio.

Work and Community

The next biggest influence outside of your friends and family is your work environment and the community in which you live. This may be a greater influence for some people than others. For people who are extremely career oriented, their business and career can dominate their internal environment. They become almost obsessed with focusing purely on moving their career forward. Others on the other hand are able to create a separation between personal and business life. I do feel, however, that with recent economic times people are bringing the stress and pressure of work more and more into their homes. This has an immediate and often negative impact on the inner world of their children and loved ones.

The community in which you live also has a significant impact on your inner world and the perception that you have of life. A child growing up in an inner-city area where there may be a high demographic of low-income families will have a very different view of the world to somebody whose family is wealthy, growing up in an affluent area.

I recommend writing the following questions in your journal and then writing the answers to each one.

> **Does this environment within which I live and work lift me up or drag me down?**
>
> **Do I feel safe and comfortable in this environment?**
>
> **Am I inspired by those around me and what I see?**
>
> **Does my working environment align with my Core Values?**
>
> **Is there a community spirit?**
>
> **Do I have the ability to contribute and give beyond myself?**

Remember the overall objective of these questions is to establish whether your external environment is serving your life and purpose in a positive way. If not – then it is probably time to make changes.

Culture, Religion and Country

You will be fully aware that some cultures are enriched with tradition more than others. Some cultures and countries have developed a lifestyle and environment based on the strong philosophies of one or more religions. The same can also be said for the dominant political influences within the country – communism and capitalism are classic examples. In the same way you have looked at family, friends, work and community, you may need to look at a broader influence that culture, religion and country have on your inner world and the outlook you have on life.

To some extent this can be even more challenging than the other influences we have discussed. Especially if you are living in a culture or even within a religious environment that you do not necessarily wholeheartedly align with. To go against the thinking of a larger group of people can almost feel impossible for some people.

Only you can decide whether the greater external environment of your culture, environment and country is serving to help you grow as a human being or not. Ask the same questions as the ones I listed above. Be a silent witness to your situation and watch how you are showing up in this world. If your environment is supporting you then that is excellent and if not, then ask the question 'Is it time to relocate?'

Is It Time To Relocate?

The process of evaluating your outer world that we have just discussed enables you to objectively decide if these influences are helping you to grow as a person and to move forward or not. It is as simple as that. You are looking to align yourself with people, places and environments that uplift you and that inspire you.

Don't get me wrong. When it comes to having the right people around you I am not saying that you want a bunch of people who simply agree with everything you say. Actually it is healthy to have people around you who can stretch you and who are not afraid to challenge you and certain beliefs as long as they are coming from a loving, non-ego driven place.

If you have identified that something in your external environment is not serving you then you will either have to develop a very strong filter mechanism so that the environment and those closest to you do not negatively impact your inner world.

Alternatively, you make the decision to completely change your external environment. In order to do this you will need to consider relocating or choosing new friends. With family this can be more complicated. In the case of family I believe it is about limiting the amount of negative experience you have with them. Which in simple terms may require you to limit the type of conversation you have with them. You simply don't allow the subjects you discuss to cross into the area that you know becomes a conflict or a negative draw down.

Anna and Honza Decide To Change Country

Two of my clients, Anna and Honza, are currently in their mid-to-late twenties. Both of them grew up in one of the Eastern bloc countries where they experienced a heavy influence from communism. When I was coaching them they explained to me how at an early age they both felt inspired to try different things in their lives. They wanted to create more financial security in order to be able to help their family. This was a philosophy that went completely against the economic ethos of the country and the community around them.

Both spoke very passionately about the challenges their family had faced. Anna's father had been a writer and on one occasion his worked was banned because in some of the articles that he had written he'd slightly questioned the philosophy of the political system. Anna and Honza received resistance about their dreams from everybody around them. By the time they reached their early twenties they realized that if they carried on living where they were living they would never achieve their dream. And so, although they loved their family very much, they made a life-changing and tough decision to physically leave their family, community and the country.

I am pleased to say that today they are very happy and are working passionately towards their dream and attracting new opportunities all the time. They have started their own business, which is now expanding, and they are now able to start sending money home to their parents. In addition, they are working with me and my business partner Raj to develop a large property portfolio.

The above example may appear extreme; however, when you are faced with overwhelming external influences, often the only way to achieve a radical change is an extreme course of action that makes the biggest impact. Even after arriving in the United Kingdom they still took a few years to adjust and work on their inner worlds because of the immense impact from the previous programming they had received for 20 years.

A change of environment is sometimes so impactful that people often wonder why they did not do it earlier. The reason people don't make the change is either because they are not aware of the influence that their external environment has upon them, or they are not experiencing enough emotional pain to make the relevant changes in their lives.

How to Change Your Environment

I believe it is time for you to consider which environments you need to change in order to move forward. Here is my suggested five-step process to clearing up or changing your environment:

1. Remove all the clutter in your immediate external world (home or one specific room) and organise it so that your working and living space feels and looks much tidier.

2. Work through the exercises in this book designed for helping you clear your Inner World (beliefs, Value Conditions and Core Values).

3. Identify the external environmental distractions around you, working outwards from family and immediate friends as described in this chapter. Where necessary, remove them, redefine the relationships or relocate yourself.

4. Write down and be clear what environment you want to have around you including the people, working environment and your geographical location. Describe on paper the type of people you want to attract into your life. What values and beliefs would you want them to have? Then put out a strong intention to

the universe that you are open to meeting the right people and finding the right place to live. Take specific action to make it happen.

5. Check-in on a weekly basis to ensure that you are maintaining the right environment and that you are improving.

This last part is very important to your personal growth. Certainly for the first few months it is important to be finely tuned in to what things lift you up or put you down. Remember you can choose to control your internal and external environments. That means if you're aware of what things motivate or drain you, you can anticipate them in advance and where necessary move away from or towards them.

9 | **Step Six** - Wake-Up On Purpose With A Vision

Introduction

This is the last and arguably the most exciting step in the Change Process – this is where you will explore your purpose and vision for your life. As I sit down to write this chapter I am faced with the fact that hundreds of authors and inspirational speakers have either written about or spoken about the importance of having a vision for your future. In fact, just for a moment, let's look at some examples:

"Here is a promise: if you make the effort to develop the habit of unusual clarity, the payoff for you down the road will be tremendous."

Jack Canfield

"Imagination can transform your physical appearance. Imagine yourself with twinkling eyes, a beaming face, a radiant personality; hold that picture in your mind and you will become that kind of person."

Robert H Schuller

"I have a dream…"

Martin Luther King

*"Once you see that your perceptions determine your
behaviour, you can begin immediately to shift your
focus from your actions to your attitudes.
When you change in your mind's eye, you see
things differently with your physical high."*

Jim Harkness and Neil Eskelin

"We become what we think about."

Earl Nightingale

I first heard this last quote some back in the early 1990s when listening to a recording called *The Strangest Secret*. Many of you reading this book will be familiar with the recent and inspiring docu-film called *The Secret*. This movie sold millions in a short space of time. Although *The Secret* has been hailed a great success and for many it has been a revelation, actually, the modern day teachings of *The Secret* stem very much from those early teachings of Earl Nightingale and Napoleon Hill who themselves brought to the public eye the message from some of the greatest philosophers of times passed. The single most important message that comes from this teaching is that we attract what we focus on with enough intent and consistency. So let's focus on your purpose.

First we'll look at attraction

The law of attraction has become almost a household term in the 21st century and yet I believe that most people do not truly apply it in a conscious way. Let me rephrase that – most people apply it all the time, but don't realise it. And ironically, they apply it the wrong way. The reason the success of *The Secret* has been so great is because we are also at a point in history when people are reaching out for a way to improve their lives and create more abundance and health. There is a massive shift that is taking place in the level of human consciousness and the teachings of *The Secret* form part of this rising consciousness.

At a quantum physical level, our thoughts do create shifts in universal energy. However, and there is a however, the reality is that in order for the vibrational harmony to occur such that the law of attraction can truly work for you, then you must take on board this philosophy at a very fundamental level. My belief is that it all starts from Intention. At your core you have a deep-rooted spiritual intention, which is the source of your attractive energy. Just for a moment, consider that word, 'intention'. Wayne Dyer made this the subject of an entire book. Deepak Chopra writes about intention in an entire chapter in one of his books called *Synchro Destiny*.

> *"All the activity in the universe is generated by intention. According to the Verdantic tradition, intent is the force of nature. It maintains the balance of all the universal elements and forces that allow the universe to continue to evolve."*
> Deepak Chopra.

If you take it to a deeper level and look at the neurological impact of a thought with a pure and focused intention, then there are patterns of individual neurons in different parts of the brain that are activated by this single intention. These thoughts create signals with a specific frequency that is tied into the cognitive process. When that thought or intention is put in place, a chain reaction occurs which results in you consciously and subconsciously taking certain actions.

Please note that this word ACTION is critical. Many think that no action is needed. I don't agree. I believe that in the experience of practicing purposeful intent, we must also act as though it has happened and follow through on a practical day-to-day basis. If you do this, you will reach what I call *The Critical Point Of Contact* between intent and attraction. You are the conduit, the interface where the two meet. At that point, it is for you to act or the moment will be lost. In simple terms, the rubber meets the road when intention and attraction align.

If you or I were to strike a musical note of a specific vibrational frequency with a tuning fork or our voice then we could actually break a glass. Equally, if you generate a very specific thought pattern with enough purpose and intention on a consistent and regular basis, with enough intensity, you will create a vibrational frequency that will resonate with that which you are looking to attract on a universal level. Think about the attraction that people like Mahatma Ghandi, Mother Teresa and Martin Luther King created. When you think how they aligned this phenomenal energy behind their intention with the purpose that they lived day-by-day then you can see how and why they were able to achieve such great things.

You will have experienced this before but maybe not been aware of it. People will turn up in your life who seem to be linked with the thing you are focusing on. Information becomes available to you that you were never aware of before that has a direct influence on you achieving your goal; or a person comes into your life that turns out to be the perfect life partner. Financial opportunities reveal themselves that potentially make your path easier. Solutions to problems that were blocking you before emerge from apparently nowhere. All these things are universally linked with the attractive forces that you put in motion. These occurrences are often called *coincidences*.

Our skill is to become aware of these occurrences and understand how to interpret them, rather than simply ignoring them or passing them off as coincidences.

Vision Is Attraction

Does this seem a little bit far-fetched? Maybe it does, especially if this is not a subject that you have ever really studied. However, the reality is that science has now reached a point where it has proven that a single thought generates emotional responses (feelings) at a cellular and bio-chemical level in our bodies. Naturally then, the greater the intent and purpose, the greater the response our body produces to that which we are thinking about and focusing on. In simple terms, the more you are on purpose, the more you focus and visualise on your purpose and the greater you will develop vibrational harmony with what you are seeking.

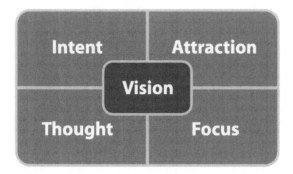

1 **Intention** is the source of your desire. This is the birthplace of your vision, an embryo in its purest form. This intention must come from a point of absolute pure desire to achieve the vision that you see in front of you.

2 **Thought** is the conscious and unconscious part of the process. This is where you start to form images and substance to the pure intention behind the thought.

3 **Focus** - For resonant harmony to occur with that which you are trying to attract, your thoughts must be focused with absolute sharpness and clarity. Also, part of the process of focusing is taking specific physical action towards that which you desire. When you focus your intention and thoughts it has the same effect as taking the sun's light and passing it through a magnifying glass. You create a sharp point where all elements come together and intense heat and energy are formed.

4 *Attraction* – Attractive forces activate once you consistently apply the first three steps described above. By keeping your vision clearly out in front of you, and continually practicing the thought and focus process, many incidences of attraction will occur. They do not always occur on a massive scale, more often than not, they happen as smaller occurrences that as a collective have a big impact. You have to have your radar working continuously to detect opportunity when it arrives.

In his book *Empires of The Mind*, Dennis Waitley describes one of his most inspiring relationships with a gentleman called Jim Stovall. Jim is the founder of the Narrative Television Network, a cable network for blind people. Jim lost his eyesight many years ago, but he has never lost his vision, his determination, or his stride. He creates programs that people can enjoy and profit from using their inner vision. This simple and beautiful description encapsulates exactly the message I would like to get across in this chapter. Your vision starts in your heart and mind.

The Critical Point of Contact

Okay, we've had a look the philosophical and semi-scientific reasoning behind the importance of creating a vision, so let's put some practical application into play. The reason I want to get you to take practical steps towards defining your vision is because it's very easy to have a nice, warm fuzzy feeling and discussion about the law of attraction. Unfortunately, just thinking about it does not produce results. Hence, we need to take action.

Let me start here with a simple analogy. Imagine that you want to take a journey from your home to visit a beautiful oceanfront destination about four hours' drive from your home. You have been on the Internet, looked at the photographs, spoken to people who have visited this location and spent time planning all the different experiences you are going to have when you arrive at this beautiful destination. The vision is clear. The level at which you desire this experience will directly influence the amount of effort you put in to getting there. Having assessed the weather forecast you discover that there's going to be a heat wave and absolutely crystal clear conditions next weekend. You can't wait to get there.

Next weekend arrives and having packed your bags you set off on your journey. Listening to the radio you hear confirmation that the weather conditions are fabulous. After just 45 minutes of driving you hit horrendous traffic conditions. It turns out that there has been a major accident which is causing a three-hour tailback. You decide to reroute using your navigator and before long you are back in the driving seat and the traffic is flowing. Half an hour later there are thick black clouds forming just ahead of you and within minutes you experience the most amazing thunderstorm and heavy rain. In fact, the rain is so heavy that it creates flash floods that block the road ahead of you. At this point you're feeling extremely frustrated, however nothing is going to stop you getting to your destination. The only way to get round this problem is to reroute a second time which now means that your total drive time will be approximately 7 hours.

Do you give up?

Is it really worth going on?

Is it easier to listen to your negative voice and turn back?

Listening to the radio there is live commentary from your destination where people are chilling out on the beach and enjoying the most amazing weather. There is also a special carnival taking place over the weekend and celebrations will go late into the night. You're excited and you still have the desire to get there. You find an alternative route and eventually after a long journey you arrive at your destination six hours later than you expected, tired but excited.

Fundamentally, whether the journey is a six-hour drive or six years of your life plan the principle is exactly the same. If you do not have clarity, excitement and passion about the life that you wish to live in the future then you will not have the inspiration to overcome the challenges that will inevitably come your way. When this happens people give up and don't bother going all the way. So the reason behind the journey has to be so strong and emotionally stimulating that giving up is not an option.

To make this simple let's break the areas of your vision into four key parts:

1. **Wealth and contribution** *(giving)*

2. **Health** *(physical and dietary)*

3. **Family & friends**

4. **Personal growth** *(spiritual, emotional and intellectual)*

If you choose to take this to another level you can actually break your life vision into many different areas that align with your value system. However, for now I suggest you keep it simple and focus on these four areas.

The process we're going to go through now should be carried out in each of these four areas. My suggestion is that you start with Health simply because your vision for the future will be most enjoyable if you are leading a healthy and vibrant lifestyle. And remember that this is your vision, not mine or anybody else's.

Creating and shaping your vision

You're probably going to need to spend several hours on this process since it must be repeated for each of the four areas described. Also I think it is important that you do not treat this as a chore. If for any reason you start to feel your energy dropping or that you are simply turning the handle as you are creating the written description of your vision, then I suggest you put the pen down and take a break. Only do this when you are 100% committed, excited and engaged with the experience. This process can take many hours and even days. I recall first doing this years ago and was so inspired that I spread the process over four days and really allowed myself to create clarity on what I wanted in the future.

> If you are currently experiencing some really challenging times in one or more areas of your life you must put aside any negative thoughts and feelings about that for the moment. This is an opportunity for you to take a deep breath and give yourself a chance to walk into the future – irrespective of what is happening now.

For the sake of this exercise we are going to imagine two to five years in the future. You can carry out this exercise for any period of time and you may choose to take a shorter goal than two years and also, you may want to consider a longer period out beyond five years. This is a five-step journey that ideally should become an ongoing process that you review regularly.

Step 1: *A journey in the mind*

You may need to read this first and then do the exercise. Find a quiet place where you can sit back, close your eyes and not be disturbed. Take three deep breaths and with each one gently let the air out whilst smiling and feeling a quiet sense of excitement about the future. Now take a further three deep breaths and this time as you're breathing out quietly on the tip of your tongue say to yourself the area of your life that you wish to create your vision for. For example, you can say to yourself 'health' or 'family'.

Imagine time stretching out in front of you as far as five years into the future. With your eyes closed, picture yourself moving rapidly into the future until you arrive at that five-year destination. As you do this, I want you to smile and imagine that you are sat strapped into a racing car seat and as you fly forward into the future you can feel yourself being pinned back into that seat.

When you arrive at your five-year destination you will become the future 'you'. This is the 'you' that is living in the future that you want. I want you to look around and really *take* in this future experience. Make the image in your mind colourful, crystal clear, and also make the sensations and the sounds amplified so that you can truly feel the experience. As you do this, practice breathing in for the count of five and then out for the count of five – continue this process, breathing deeper into your belly area.

Now I want you to focus in on a chosen area for this visualisation – for example Health. Observe your healthy lifestyle, notice little everyday things that you are doing by being this healthy person. Make mental notes so you can write these down when you open your eyes. Allow time to skip along through the day so you can observe other things about your lifestyle in this area. Imagine this is a DVD and you can fast forward or rewind and even pause when necessary.

The objective in this visualisation is to pick up lots of detail so that you can write these down into a very clear description of your vision.

Here are some simple questions for gathering information for each of the four areas of your life in your future vision:

How does it look on a daily and weekly or even hourly basis?

How do you feel inside about yourself and your life?

How do you act – your confidence and communication with others?

How do others act toward you with this new amazing life that you are leading?

What sort of things are you doing on a daily basis?

What are you excited about?

If you were to describe this person's life that you are watching what would you say about them?

We will expand on these questions further in this section, however these seven questions help focus you on what to be aware of as you observe and mentally record your lifestyle of your future vision.

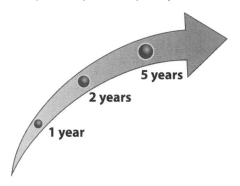

Once you have gained what you believe is sufficient clarity on this vision of your future, then take a deep breath and open your eyes. Stand up and stretch with a smile on your face. Drink at least two glasses of water. Go outside and get some fresh air and keep reflecting on what you have just seen in your mind.

Step 2: *Get it on paper*

Keeping the images clear and vivid in your mind open your journal and put the title of the subject area that you are focusing on at the top of the page. I suggest one of two main approaches:

1. Write down the answers to the previous questions. Be very specific in what you write down. Be BOLD here. Be prepared to write down big, powerful and motivating goals and aspirations. You must always bear in mind that the law of attraction works in a very powerful way and so the more specific you can be the more accurately this intention will manifest itself in the future. If you decide to use this approach, then the answers from these questions will be used to create a written description of your vision.

2. If you feel that the vision was extremely clear for you and you are comfortable with simply expressing it then you can jump straight in and start to describe your vision. Again, be explicit. Express what you are feeling, what you see and what you hear with as much clarity and detail as possible. Also remember to write down what you are excited about in this future life.

Just to help you in this process, let's take a closer look at each of the areas that you will be creating a vision for. I have created more questions for you to consider. You don't have to try and memorise them, simply be aware of them and let your subconscious mind process them.

Health

How do you want your food prepared?

Will you prepare and cook food yourself or will somebody else do it?

Will you eat out a lot or more at home?

What type of drinks will you drink?

Will you be eating organic food?

What type of exercise will you do?

How will you exercise for aerobic fitness?

How will your body look?

Will you have your own gym?

How will your energy levels be?

How will you know that you feel healthier and fitter?

Wealth & Contribution (Giving)

How much will you be earning on a monthly basis?

How much money will you have in investments?

Will your income be passive, active or a mixture of both?

What job or career will you be in?

Where will you be living?

How many homes will you own?

Where would you travel to?

What businesses will you own?

Will you own properties and shares?

Will you be fully retired?

How will your typical working day or week be?

What percentage of your income will you contribute?

What charities would you be contributing to?

Will you run your own not-for-profit business?

Family & Friends

How much time do you want to spend with your family?

How many kids would you have?

Where would you like to travel with your family?

What small and big things would you do for your family?

What fun experiences would you like to have with your friends?

What type of friends will you have around you?

What magic moments would you like to create for your family and friends?

How will it feel to spend quality time with your family whenever you want?

Will you be married?

How exciting and passionate will your marriage or relationship be?

What schools would you like your children to go to?

Will you have private tuition for your children?

What treats and relaxation will you and your partner experience together?

Personal Growth

> *How will you be pursuing your key purposes in life?*
>
> *What new subjects will you be learning?*
>
> *What seminars will you attend?*
>
> *What type of books will you be reading?*
>
> *What adventures will you go on around the world?*
>
> *What would your spiritual perspective on life be?*
>
> *How will you have matured as a human being?*
>
> *How will you feel inside about the world?*
>
> *How will others view you and how you show up in the world?*
>
> *What subjects will you be passionate about?*
>
> *How will you be with your children?*
>
> *What lessons will you be sharing with your children and friends?*
>
> *How will you continue to stretch yourself?*
>
> *What type of audio programs and educational DVDs would you be watching?*
>
> *How often will you be meditating?*
>
> *How will you express gratitude in your life?*

Step 3: *Review and Calibrate*

This may sound like an odd step; however, it is actually an important part of the process. Having written down in your words, your vision for each of the different areas of your life, the next step is to read over what you have written. The objective here is to measure or calibrate your internal reaction to what you have written. Put in a more spiritual and energetic way – does it resonate with you?

One important message here, 'get out of your head'. Let me say this again, 'get out of your head'. This was a challenge I had for a long time. If you try and intellectualise this exercise it will not work. The objective here is to become part of the experience to such an extent that you feel what it would be like for you in your future body five years from today. If what you have written does not really connect in an emotional, inspirational and resonant way, then rewrite it until it does.

Something that works for a lot of people is to create what many call a Vision Board. I prefer to call it a Reality Board. This is a large sheet of paper or picture frame onto which you stick photographs and images of the lifestyle that you will be living and that you wish to attract to you. This vision can also reflect your purpose and how you want to add value to the world. Have fun with this process. Get clear and vivid pictures. It works. When you do this and reflect on these images you literally find yourself focusing on the activities needed to make them a reality.

Step 4: *Look At It Regularly*

This amazing vision that you are writing down is not supposed to be tucked away in a drawer and pulled out once every year. Actually, this is something that happens to a majority of people that set goals and create written vision statements. This is also a habit that I developed in my early days of doing this back in the 1980s. I would spend hours really describing how I wanted my life to be and I would also create images from photographs to develop a vision board (which is something I would also recommend you do). I would be very excited about the vision and my vision board and then I would put it away and forget to review it. By not reading my own vision on a regular basis I was not creating the thought process and the focus to allow the law of attraction to work in my favour. Only by changing this habit was I able to really make significant changes in my life. The more I started to reflect on my vision(s) and the images on my Reality Board the more I found the opportunities appeared in front of me. All the things that I have in my life were all written down on paper years ago.

The key here is to develop a habit. Whether you review your vision statements and Reality Board in the morning or in the evening is entirely up to you. The important thing is that you do review them and do it with a warm, open and happy heart.

Step 5: *Look for signs*

This is an essential step in the process – you must keep your radar out to spot certain signs. Once you are aligned with your vision and you are regularly reflecting on where you want to be, your radar must be ready to receive. Signs can come in many different forms and over time you will become more and more experienced at identifying them.

What do I mean by signs? Signs could be in the form of a conversation with somebody who happens to mention that they have a friend who specialises in an area that is exactly what you need at that moment in your life to achieve part of your vision. Another sign could be when you bump into somebody at a social event who just happens to run a business, and they are developing new products that tie into the business that you are developing for the future. It could be that you are looking to write a book as I was, and a friend who knows you well happens to spot an advert for a book coach and they pass on the advert to you which is exactly what happened to me. The key is to act on such opportunities.

Signs can also be warnings that you are going in the wrong direction. This has happened to me a few times in my life. I was pushing hard on money-related opportunities in one area of my life and yet I was experiencing personal challenges in other areas and it did not make sense. Then, when I stopped and really looked, it became clear that these challenges were signals trying to slow me down and even stop me from pursuing these other money-related projects. These were projects that actually had nothing to do with my real purpose or passion, and that is what I interpreted as the message – 'get back on track, Rohan, and stop chasing the money here.' In other words, if you experience a shock or specific extreme stress in one area of your life, take a look around to see if it is a possible sign from the universe telling you to consider whether this or something else you are doing is out of alignment with your life path. When I really understood this, it changed the whole way I looked at the world.

So when things happen, even the tiniest incidences, take a moment to check in to see if there is a sign here, and if so, decide what actions need to be taken. At the same time be wary of trying to read into everything that happens around you. You need to be sensitive to the possibility of a message but not obsessed with finding one. I am simply saying, use these signs as a chance to pause, reflect and where necessary adjust. Most importantly, enjoy the journey.

Are You On Purpose?

This is a subject that could fill a whole book. Should I have a life purpose? What the heck is a life purpose? How do I find my purpose? These are all valid questions that people have asked me over the years.

What the heck is a life purpose?

I will tell you what the meaning of *purpose* is to me in the context of the message I am sharing in this book. Firstly I actually believe that each of us can, and often do, have more than one purpose in life. However, I also believe that in each of us there is something deep down that we are more passionate about than anything else. This is what I call your Life Purpose; others may refer to it as their *calling*. This is often a way of living, a role you may have, something that you do that makes you feel totally inspired and alive – it is your place in this world where you just flow effortlessly and wake up every morning excited about being in that place.

When someone is on purpose they are like a magnet attracting people and opportunities to them. Their whole life is guided by a message they need to share, a family they want to bring up and care for, an invention they have yet to discover, a painting they have to create, songs they want to sing, mountains they want to climb, a business they want to build or lives they want to save. They do not allow themselves to be distracted from their course. These people all live or have lived a life on purpose – Mahatma Gandhi, Mother Teresa, Nelson Mandela, Abraham Lincoln, John F Kennedy, Maya Angelou.

I want to add here that you can also have a purpose around each of the areas that are important in your life. When you do this, it makes things clearer for you on a day-to-day basis and helps you identify which area of your life you are less and more inspired by. So in the area of health you can have a purpose to how you live your life or in relationships you can have a purpose behind how you want to show up in this area. I will illustrate with a personal example shortly.

Should I have a life purpose?

The simple answer to this in my opinion is yes. But that does not mean I am right. I have simply found that people with a purpose and a vision for the future are happier and more excited about life. Can your purpose change? Absolutely. I was privileged that my purpose revealed itself to me in my early thirties. I discovered that I have a message to share and a gift to be able to share it. Speaking and writing gives me a vehicle to deliver my message. Could that change? Yes. For now I am passionate about living this journey and maybe, as the years pass, the direction and focus of what inspires me may change.

The other massive purpose for me is my own family and that is equally a strong guiding light for how I live my life. I would simply add here that if you are waking up in the mornings feeling a sense of frustration and saying to yourself there must be more to life than this, then it is highly likely that you are not aligning with your vision and purpose.

How Do I Find My Purpose?

I am not convinced that you should search for your purpose. I believe that it will more often than not reveal itself to you by the messages and signs that you receive along the way. To help you with this, if I were mentoring you now I would ask questions like:

When do you feel most alive and what are you doing when you feel that way?

What have you done in the past that has inspired you?

Who inspires you in the world and what do they do?

What have other people told you about your purpose and when do you appear to be inspired and alive from their perspective?

Life leaves clues. The important thing is to go back to your childhood and let go of your logical brain. Think about what excited you and what you wanted to be and do. Look for signs that are common and that come up again several times. The clues will be there; just allow them to reveal themselves.

Finally, the exercise we did at the start of the chapter was about vision. Your vision and passion are often closely aligned which is also why I wanted you to do the exercise. In your ideal vision for the future, there will be a clue about what your purpose is. It could be working with a charity, educating others, writing books, working the land, being an amazing parent, creating wealth and helping others do the same. Allow your vision to reveal these clues.

Defining Your Purpose

In each of the key areas of my life I like to have a written description of how I want to show up in that area and what I believe my purpose in that particular part of my life is. Doing this really helps me stay clear on what it means to me to be healthy, or a great family man or a successful entrepreneur. I would like to share an example and hope that it will inspire you to explore some of the areas of your life where you could develop a stronger purpose.

What I recommend is that your purpose should have at least four elements to it:

1. *It should allow you to contribute to the world in some way*

2. *It must be uplifting and incorporate inspirational words*

3. *It must give you a huge sense of personal satisfaction when you think of it*

4. *It should allow you to grow and expand as a person*

In the area of my vision and purpose as an Inspirational Speaker and Teacher here is my purpose statement.

> To help people around the world to achieve their dreams, spreading love and laughter into people's lives. Help people make powerful, rapid and uplifting changes. To constantly be developing myself and sharing tools for making unbelievable and lasting change. To help children grow with a vision of a beautiful and fulfilling future. To create special-inspirational moments that remain in people's memories for the rest of their lives. To move people emotionally and spiritually. To spread a message of global philanthropy. To be an outstanding motivator and life changer. To be recognised as a leading light and one of the world's most inspiring messengers.

Hopefully you can see that when I have this vision and purpose close to my heart I am inspired to speak and help others no matter what my circumstances are. If, like me, you have similarly inspiring written statements in each of the key areas your life, you will find yourself waking up and living every day on purpose.

Congratulations

It is now officially time to celebrate as you have finished the Six Step Change Process. The whole journey is about continued growth and discovering how you can apply these tools on a daily basis to both your life and those around you. Revisit this process or different elements of it whenever you feel the need to make adjustments in your life.

The next section in the book has been written to address the three main areas where people experience the most challenges in their lives. Each chapter is designed to provide you with tools and insights in to how to create positive and purposeful change in your Health, Finances and Relationships.

The Three Pillars
For Life Balance

10 | Health - Live A Vibrant and Healthy Life

Introduction

From the personal surveys that I have carried out with audiences and clients around the world, Health, Vitality and Fitness have ranked in the top three key areas that people want to improve. I hear them say that they feel stressed, overweight, unfit, low on energy, fuzzy in their thinking, emotionally drained, apathetic and that they seem to get sick and develop colds quite regularly. I am not saying all these happen at the same time, although in some cases they do – the point is that I believe these are all a symptom of poor health and fitness. The great news is that from my own experience, I believe that you can stop this through some basic diet and health-related steps.

Around 300BC, Herophilus was supposed to have said that *'to lose one's health renders science null, art inglorious, strength unavailing, wealth useless and eloquence powerless.'* Centuries later, these words could not be more true. No matter how hard you work or how much you earn, if you feel unfit and apathetic, then what was the point of it all in the first place?

You will hopefully recall that in reviewing my hierarchy of Core Values, I moved Health and Fitness to the top of my list. This may be something you have to consider very carefully. My reason for including a specific chapter in the book on health is simple; if you are currently facing any kind of issue or challenge in your life and your health and vitality are out of balance then this will have an immediate impact on your emotional strength and stamina. When you are feeling energised and vibrant, you are able to take on issues and challenges that might stop you in your tracks when you are unhealthy and apathetic.

So my intention here is to firstly help you gain clarity on your existing beliefs around health and then to look at how you want to feel in your ideal world. We will then go through the initial steps to start that process of change. I believe that this will have a knock-on effect in every area of your life.

There is one other reason for including this subject in the book – I would like you to live a long and healthy life.

So what is your personal goal?

Without great health and vitality, virtually every other area of your life will be experienced at a mediocre level. Ultimately you must be the one that defines your goals for your health, not me nor anyone else. There are massive benefits to changing what you eat and drink and the level of exercise that you do. From my experience and observations, I have found that all of the following benefits are achievable with a change of diet and fitness. The following table will help you get clarity on specifically which area you would like to improve.

Your Primary Goal	Yes (✓) or No (X)
Increase your energy levels	
Improved immune system and fewer illnesses	
Help to cure common ailments and illnesses	
Eliminate physical apathy and laziness	
Increase alertness and focus	
Increased passion	

Your Primary Goal	Yes (✓) or No (X)
Increase vitality	
Lose or gain weight naturally	
Improved skin tone and complexion	
Wake up earlier, feel more alive on less sleep	
Have a clearer and more alert mind	
Get fitter and feel more toned	

I have personally experienced or witnessed every single one of the above benefits through the simple process of changing and sticking to a more life-enhancing diet. It works and there are thousands of people who stand testament to this.

Previously I mentioned that often when we experience a significant emotional event it changes our beliefs about the world. In my case, my beliefs about diet were massively changed in 2002 when we discovered that my mother had cancer.

What I would like to share with you is my experience of what happened. There are many forms of cancer and illness and the reason I am sharing with you is so that you get to see firsthand how my understanding and belief system of health and diet were radically shaped. It is not meant to provide a medical solution to a health challenge that you or someone you know may be experiencing. In this respect you should seek the guidance of a specialist or doctor. I do, however, hope that it will make you stop and seriously think about the impact of diet on your overall health.

My Mum's Story – Cancer

I would like to expand more on my mum's story. In 2002 we discovered that my mother had cancer of the womb and cervix. The doctors appeared to be indicating that there were several approaches that could be used including a drug-based option.

Having already become aware of the massive benefits of diet change and mind-set have on cancer I was compelled to study this further to see what the modern-day research had discovered about non-drug-related ways to reduce or beat cancer.

Many of the studies I read shocked me and excited me. I read case after case of people who had reduced cancerous tumours by simply cutting out certain foods and adding life-enhancing types of food. Having discovered this, I sat with my mother and explained all that I had read. Eventually, after much discussion she agreed to follow my suggestions.

We stopped her eating meat, dairy products, acid-forming foods, tea and coffee and alcohol. She kept on this for several months. She lost weight in a natural way, her energy went up, her hair seemed to look healthier and people even commented on how well she looked.

Subsequent visits to the doctors and scans revealed that she was not going to need the use of drugs and that aside from one minor operation to remove a very small remaining area of cancer, she was in great health. The doctors even told her to keep doing what she was doing.

Eight years later, as my mum approaches 70 years of age, she is alive and well, has three granddaughters and is cancer free. It is still my belief that the changes we implemented in her diet played a massive role in the process of her body healing.

You can see how my beliefs were redefined by this one experience. In fact, at the same time that mum changed her diet we were doing exactly the same. I have maintained 80% of it and modified the other 20% where necessary based on new discoveries about diet, longevity of life and vitality. My goal in this chapter is to share with you an insight into that very same diet. I will add that I have shared that story on many occasions to live audiences and have attendees who have experienced very similar results with other forms of illness. These stories continue to inspire me to share the message of the impact of diet on our health and vitality.

All that said, it is important to not rush your body. You need to allow it to respond, which means for some people, the benefits I have listed above may happen quickly and for others it may take anything from 3 to 90 days or more in some cases. Remember, if you have had toxins building up in your organs, skin, blood and joints for years, then you also have to allow the body to eliminate them through the detox process. The benefits will be huge and I mean huge. To help facilitate this process, it is essential to drink lots of water (not tap water – good quality mineral or filtered water). In doing so, you will allow bodily toxins to be flushed out.

Sadly, many people start on a new life-enhancing diet, feel the difference and get themselves feeling healthier only to 'slip off the wagon' over time. All the more reason to create powerful beliefs and values around health so that you raise your standards and don't allow yourself to be distracted.

Four Simple Elements For Improving Your Health

Remember that your mission is to increase your ability to be able to deal with current and future challenges in life, to feel healthier and more vibrant. The purpose of this chapter is to give you the tools to do that. Since this is such a vast subject I want to keep the formula for improving your health, vitality and fitness simple as possible. I believe there are four key elements that work together to create dramatic effects on your state of health. I will focus in on the dietary elements for the purpose of this chapter.

Exercise

Detox and Cleanse

Live and Super Foods

Hydrate (water)

I know you are probably thinking that this looks too simple or there must be more to it than that – actually it really isn't. Don't get me wrong, there are many layers to each of these which you will discover on your journey to maximum health and vitality.

Detox and Cleanse

People do get confused by the terms Detox and Cleanse and they can often be treated as the same. In some respects they do ultimately help to serve the same purpose, which is to remove toxic waste from your body. However, I would like to give you a simple understanding of the two. When you go through a Detox, you are going through a diet-related process that aims at eliminating toxins that have built up in your body which includes your blood and organs.

When you go through a Cleanse you typically can use diet supplements and semi-intrusive methods of clearing different parts of your digestive tract. For most people, the most common forms of cleanse includes anything from simply drinking herbal-based drinks to colonic-hydrotherapy. You literally can clean from the top and the bottom.

Why Do You Need to Detox and Cleanse?

Throughout our lives our bodies build up toxic deposits in our blood, cells, joints and organs as a result of what we eat, our environment and even our stress levels. If these are not removed (detox and cleansed), then they can develop into degenerative type diseases and ailments that show up at different stages of your life depending on how toxic you are. With a toxic system your immune system lowers and you become much more susceptible to common ailments like colds and flus.

Actually our body is a magnificent creation that in theory has all the resources built in to detox and cleanse. This is done through the lymphatic system, lungs, kidneys, blood, colon, skin and the liver. Under normal operating circumstances, eating in moderation and without the modern day pressures and environmental changes, these seven systems should work well. However, the rapidly growing statistics of degenerative diseases and every-day illnesses suggests otherwise.

Also part of the build-up of toxins is the development of free radicals in our bodies. It is widely accepted in the medical world that having an excess of free radicals produces harmful oxidation that can damage cell membranes and cause accelerated ageing and facilitate the development of degenerative diseases. On the US National Cancer Institute website they state the following: "Antioxidants are substances that may protect cells from the damage caused by unstable molecules known as free radicals. Free radical damage may lead to cancer." The contributing factors that cause an excess of free radicals can include the following:

+ *Poor quality diet*

+ *Fried foods*

+ *Tobacco smoke*

+ *Chemicals in the home or at work*

+ *Pollution and Radiation*

+ *Alcohol*

+ *Excessive amounts of sunlight*

+ *High-fat diet*

+ *Insecticides*

+ *Stress*

+ *Insufficient sleep*

Therefore your goal should be to minimize the exposure to these through simple changes in your lifestyle and diet.

Detoxing Made Easy

A detox involves you stopping putting toxins into your body and by replacing a poor quality diet with good hydration and natural foods – in doing this you will flush the toxins out of your body. The initial stage is to reduce certain foods that you are aware can create toxic build up and at the same time replace them with a healthier alternative.

Here are some suggestions for toxic and life-enhancing foods and environments.

Food That May Create Toxins	Healthier Foods/Drinks To Try
Tea, Coffee, Soda drinks, Sweet drinks	Mineral & lemon water, fresh juices, supergreens
Fatty food	Fresh Whole-food, More greens and salads
Poor quality cooked meats	Live natural greens and similar
Sweet cakes and similar foods	Organic Raw alternatives – date and honey-based
Refined sugars	Natural fruits
Processed breads	Sprout bread, dehydrated alternatives, flat bread
Processed canned food	Raw, steamed fresh vegetables
Alcohol	Natural drink alternatives, anti-oxidant juices
Over stress	Meditate and relax
Polluted environment	Get out into some clean fresh air

When you go through this experience you will notice certain signs that toxins are coming out of your body. You will need to allow 3 to 90 days for your body to expel many of the toxins in your system. During this process it is important to keep drinking lots of clean water. This will help your body remove the toxins. The things you will notice include spots on your skin, bad breath, boils, stronger smelling urine, headaches, being irritable, massive drop in energy, diarrhoea and more.

This may sound unpleasant, but remember there are years of toxic build-up coming out here and for the first week or so you may actually feel worse – which is why so many people give up.

Juice Fast

Ideally, if you are open to doing it, a juice fast is a very effective way to really accelerate the detoxification process. I have done many of these over the years and they leave you feeling lighter, cleaner and much sharper in your thinking. Juice fasting is simply living on only freshly made juices from anything from a day to a week or more. The best way to start is to do it for a day first. This allows your body to only receive good quality nutrition without having to work hard to digest it. Over several days, the detoxing systems in the body are not over loaded with other toxic food coming in and hence you are able to release a lot of toxic waste.

Your juices should ideally be freshly made and include vegetables and some fruits – although on our juice fasts we only have limited fruits to avoid a sugar overload in the blood. Juices can include:

+ *Cucumber*
+ *Celery*
+ *Ginger*
+ *Water and Superfoods*
+ *Courgettes*
+ *Sprouted seeds like alfalfa*
+ *Carrots*
+ *Spinach*
+ *Apple*
+ *Avocado*

Aim to drink a few glasses of clean water in the morning when you rise to allow the system to flush the toxins out early and keep drinking throughout the day. Lemon squeezed into the water has an added benefit we will cover later. If you have some time watch the videos on my YouTube channels or blog of a live cleanse I did whilst staying in Denmark in July 2010.

Cleansing: Top Down – Bottom Up

There is a big cross over with Cleansing and Detoxing when we consider the dietary element simply because much of what you eat and drink during the detox has an automatic cleansing effect. Where there is a big difference is when you consider colonic hydrotherapy.

In your body you have a lymphatic system that basically acts as a toxic waste drainage system. Toxins from the blood vessels pass into the lymphatic system and get carried to the lymph nodes where there is toxic break down and a release of toxins out of the body. The fluid-pumping action of the lymphatic system is accelerated by movement of the body. Therefore, during a cleanse, if you are able to move up and down, bounce on your toes or jog a little it will help move the toxic fluids around and out of your body. This is all essential to your overall cleansing process and should be done even when not on a cleanse.

Bottoms Up

You probably smiled when you saw the title, but the process is literally that, a flushing process from your bottom up. I have to say from a personal perspective, I have found this process both relaxing, relieving and once it is finished, one feels genuinely cleansed at a much deeper level.

When you eat a poor quality, low-fluid-intake diet with toxic foods like those listed in the previous table, you develop sticky faecal matter in your colon. If your body does not eliminate these deposits effectively, then these deposits build up on the inside walls of the colon and form hard faecal matter. Not pleasant. The danger becomes worse when this hard matter starts to decay and as a result, bacteria and poisons release into the body and in extreme cases become the start of colon cancer or other colon-related diseases.

The great news is that through a gentle cycling of warm water up through the rectum and around your colon, these hard faecal deposits can be flushed out. Modern day colonic hydrotherapy uses a very small, barely noticeable process that, once you have relaxed into it, takes around 30 to 45 minutes per session. From my own personal experience, it is much more effective to go for colonic sessions after you have been on a detox and juice fast for about two to three days so that you stomach is basically empty. Then maintain the fast for a week if you can and have another one or two colonic sessions during the juice fast. I would highly recommend taking the time to research this.

Hydrate

The message here is simple, stay hydrated on a consistent basis and you will feel better, have a clearer head and most importantly, it will support your body in the normal elimination processes that takes place every day.

Depending on what sources you read the human body is about 70% - 80% water. In fact, certain organs, like your brain and your blood are over 80% water. Water helps in so many ways, not least the process of hydrating your blood and its cells and in the process of removal of toxins from the body. Imagine a thick build up of toxin in your blood and body tissues because they can't flush out. That is what happens when you are dehydrated. One of the reasons you get headaches is because toxins build up and cannot flush and in turn the toxins become concentrated and cause headaches.

My view is this. Water is the purest form of liquid we can drink and taken in its most natural state i.e. mineral or spring water, I believe that aside from the hydration benefits, there are also natural minerals that help sustain our bodily functions. I therefore am an advocate of drinking lots of water. If you are a tea, coffee or soda drink drinker – think of water as the flush that will help remove some of the toxins contained in these drinks.

Eat Live and Superfoods

My intention is not to tell you what you should or should not eat. The key is to go with what feels right for you having given yourself a chance to explore different options.

In this section I would like to explain the benefits of:

✦ *Eating alkalising raw and energising foods*

✦ *Supplementing your diet with superfoods*

The process of eating a high percentage of these food types aligns with the process of detoxing and cleansing discussed in the previous section.

I have friends that have 100% of their diet as raw and alkalising foods. My goal is to eat around 75% or more of my diet raw and alkalizing with the addition of superfoods to massively help my immune system and add more enzymes to my system. If I do not achieve this goal, I don't beat myself up. There are certain foods and meals that I really enjoy and that don't fall inside this overall philosophy. However, I also know that it is important to enjoy the process of eating. Therefore, on the occasions when I don't eat live, raw, alkalizing foods, I relax and know that I also juice cleanse regularly and through the rest of my diet will create balance.

The benefits if you stay close to the above diet model include raised energy, a natural loss of weight if you are currently overweight and an increase in weight if you are underweight, more vitality, better skin and an overall feeling of health.

Eating Alkalising Live Foods

I first became aware of acid-forming and alkalizing foods when I was researching ways to help my mum with her cancer. What I discovered was that if the body is constantly acidic through poor diet, it literally becomes fatigued, our immune system drops and we develop ailments, which show up in many forms.

The key is therefore to eat food that helps alkalise the body. Foods that tend to create acid in the body include alcohol, tea and coffee, refined and processed foods, bread, pasta, dairy products, meat and eggs (as listed in the previous table). On the other side, examples of foods that alkalise your blood and help increase your natural energy are listed in the table below.

Foods That Are Alkalising for the Blood

✦ Many Raw foods	✦ Lime
✦ Green Cabbage	✦ Lemon
✦ Spinach	✦ Avocado
✦ Leeks	✦ Sprouted radish
✦ Water Cress	✦ Broccoli
✦ Barley Grass	✦ Cucumber
✦ Wheat Grass	✦ Coconut water
✦ Celery	✦ Fresh Soya beans
✦ Lettuce	✦ Tomato
✦ Garlic	✦ Carrot
✦ Turnip	✦ Alfalfa grass

The types of foods that are helpful in this respect include raw foods, fresh and organic foods, water and green vegetables. I am not going to talk to about the Raw Food Diet in this book although it is a subject I have become passionate about. However, I will say that there is more and more evidence to support the massive value that a raw food diet, or high percentage of raw food diet, has on our body.

Eating Superfoods

The term 'superfoods' has become more popular since the mid 2000s and is slowly finding its way into the household language. Hopefully, that awareness curve will increase dramatically over the next few years. Superfoods are made up of a specific group of highly nutritious and edible plants that in their own right might not be classified as a food. They are considered to be an incredibly concentrated and nutrient-rich natural source that can be harvested in an organic and raw fashion. Superfoods can provide you with all your mineral and vitamin requirements. They increase vitality, sex drive, boost your immune system and at the same time provide a cleaning and alkalising effect on the body. Plus, if you are a sports person, they provide all the protein requirements you might have together with all the fatty acids that your body needs. Superfoods are literally a whole food in themselves.

The practical results that have been observed by people taking superfoods includes natural weight loss, improved hair and nails, nourishment for muscle, bone and bodily organs together with natural detoxing that happens anyway as a consequence of taking them.

What I love about taking superfoods is the ease in which they can be added to a meal or simply popped into a blender and taken with a juice or a smoothie. In one glass, you can literally have a loaded meal with every mineral, phytonutrient, vitamin and enzyme that you need. On this last point, it is worth noting that they are also considered to be the most enzyme-rich food type found in a natural form and therefore, they must be eaten in a raw uncooked state for your body to get the maximum benefit.

Typical superfoods include Bee Pollen, Acai Berry, Goji Berries, Blue Green Algae, Coconut Oil and Spirulina to name but a few. The form in which I personally take my superfoods is through juices, smoothies, raw dairy-free desserts and sometimes added to my raw food meals on a daily basis.

The starting point is to try one of the superfoods above and add it to your breakfast routine. By definition a raw product is anything that is heated to below 40°C although depending on the food type this figure could be up to 46°C. Your superfoods will come in a sealed pack, powdered, raw and ready to mix with your other food, smoothies or juices.

Word Of Warning

Some people when they start on superfoods find they experience some of the same symptoms as though they are detoxing. Several of the people I have coached through this process have called after a few days and said they have a headache or they are going to the toilet more regularly. This is the body letting go of built-up poisons. The key is to drink lots of water and give it 3 to 5 days to clear the system.

Conclusion

A busy lifestyle can be an easy reason to avoid taking the time to eat the right food. The key is to have a strong reason and purpose behind why you want to eat healthier and feel more vibrant. I hope that this chapter has generated an interest in you to explore the subject of live, raw, alkalising foods and to try some basic cleansing and detoxing. I can assure you that if you do, you will notice the benefits over a matter of a few weeks.

11 | **Relationships**
- Create An Intimate And
Passionate Relationship

Introduction

**Irrespective of whether you are single or in a relationship –
heterosexual or non-heterosexual, this chapter applies to you.
For most people, enjoying great health and wealth becomes
truly satisfying when this is experienced with an intimate, loving
partner. This may not be the case for all; however, for most people
enjoying a great relationship is an essential ingredient to their
happiness. Sadly the divorce rates appear to be climbing and
modern-day lifestyles, social pressures and stereotypes appear to
work against many couples.**

If you are either single or currently in a relationship and are looking
to experience an amazing, or even more amazing, passionate, intimate
and spiritually connected relationship, then this chapter has some
great insights for you that are rarely taught in the public domain.

I have personally experienced a journey of joy, pain and happiness
in the area of relationships. I have experienced marriage and divorce,
so I know what it means and feels like to go through that experience. I
also believe strongly that these experiences teach us invaluable lessons
about who were are at our core and the patterns we tend to exhibit
in our relationships. When challenges occur and relationships end,
some people simply get bitter, angry or frustrated and do not see

that they will have contributed partly or wholly to the cause of the problem. They look to blame their partner and end up continuing the same patterns again and again in future relationships. On the other hand, more enlightened people learn and grow from these challenges, identify their weaknesses and strengths, and then go on to have better and more fulfilling relationships in the future.

I was privileged to meet an amazing human being and a beautiful woman with whom I have been able to grow and develop a passionate and inspiring relationship. We have had our challenges along the way, especially at the start of our relationship because of 'past baggage' that we both brought into the relationship. I learned quickly that I had to align my masculine core and release my old relationship habits. And so we made a conscious choice to grow together and understand each other and learn about the dynamics that make up an exciting and fulfilling relationship. Ten years along our journey we still continue to grow and love each other passionately. Our daughter has brought us even more joy and an opportunity to experience new areas of growth both as a couple and as parents. Over these 10 years we have also been privileged to coach and help many other couples and single people and so I would like to share some of those insights with you here.

Where Are You Now?

I don't know if you are reading this as a single person looking to be part of a passionate, loving and exciting relationship; or you may be in a great relationship and wanting to make it even more exciting or possibly your relationship has *lost* something and you are wanting to improve it and create more excitement, passion and intimacy that you used to have when you first met. Equally, you may be like the lady who recently emailed me to ask whether she should leave her husband or not because the relationship has reached what she called *"a point of no return"* and as she said *"I just want to get out now."*

Firstly, if you are experiencing relationship issues right now, then the first thing to do is to put all blame aside. This chapter is not about blame or about finding tools that you can use to go back to your partner and say, *"look what it says here, this is what you need to do – I told you so."* I laugh as I write this because I have experienced and witnessed this over the years! Read this chapter with an open heart and a desire to be a better person in your relationship or future relationship.

Remember to first see your situation as it is now, not worse or better – simply as it is. Write it down and clearly state what you are seeking for yourself and your relationship. This can include being single and looking to attract the right partner for you.

If you are in a challenged relationship and you are considering breaking up or separating then with my hand on my heart, I would say to you knowing what I know now, and what I would like share with you in this book – *don't do anything rash right now – wait.* Before you do anything, read this chapter and apply what you read in this chapter along with all that you have learnt in this book to both your life and your relationship. Give yourself and your partner another chance to see if these changes will create a new fresh start where you can both explore each other in a new, exciting and different way. Give yourself that chance.

The Four Levels of Commitment and Intimacy

Over the years I have experienced and witnessed relationships that start out exciting and passionate and then over time appear to either deteriorate or slip into a mundane routine. There are others that grow and thrive and last for decades and occasionally for a lifetime. These can be categorised into four levels of relationship.

Level 1: *I'm in it for me* – this type of relationship is about taking. One or both of the partners are in some way emotionally closed, maybe even hurt from previous relationships and simply enter the relationship to get what they want physically and/or emotionally. In these relationships, you are usually left empty, unfulfilled and hurt.

Level 2: *Financial dependency* – this is the more conventional relationship in the sense that there is a practical dependency by one of the partners. Traditionally this was the woman although this has changed in modern times. The two bring something to the relationship, usually one tends to be the provider and although it may not be the most passionate and dynamic relationship, each gets what they want. These relationships often break down if the provider is unable to earn or create stability in the relationship.

Level 3: *The modern day balanced couple* – this is a couple that meet and initially have a strong, passionate connection. They stay together and roles form, tasks get shared in the day-to-day activities of their life. Patterns are created in everything they do from bathing to eating, sleeping positions in the bed to food shopping. They share the finances and there is a mutual benefit to both by being in the relationship. Their love life tends to lose its spark, they accommodate each other and the focus shifts from each other to 'things' that they can buy, a new Mercedes, a new flat screen TV or a holiday. They both know something is now missing but neither really bothers to address it.

Level 4: *I give myself completely and live with passion* – this is a couple that are able to focus not on their own personal needs but on the needs of their partner. They love unconditionally in the relationship. Each person is open to trying new things, exploring sexuality and intimacy without agenda or ego. There is a deeper spiritual connection that goes beyond the physical. Even in times of hurt and heated discussions, these couples remain in a place of love. Yes there will be challenges and emotional ups and downs, however, they understand that only by getting out of their heads, putting their egos aside can they grow and move on. At Level 4, there is no fear in the relationship, only fun, love, openness, passion and adventure. At this level in the relationship there is a higher consciousness.

Exercise - Have Honest and Open Discussion

Having read this far, I am hoping that if you are in a relationship that you are able to make an assessment of which of the four levels your relationship tends to operate at most of the time. Naturally it will fluctuate, but there will be one level that it operates at more than the others.

This following process involves you sitting down with your loved one and having an open-hearted discussion about your relationship. If they have not read this book, ask them to simply read the section above on the four levels. If they are open to this, ask them at what level they believe you both operate in the relationship. Then take some time to discuss the following (it may take several hours or even days of different discussions). Irrespective of whether you have been together for weeks or years, this a fantastic voyage of discovery. Don't just give one sentence answers, keep going and asking 'what else?' 'What else?'

> *What are you truly looking for in a relationship?*
>
> *What qualities do you love most in a partner?*
>
> *What excites you most?*
>
> *What turns you on?*
>
> *What do I do that bugs you?*
>
> *What do I do that you really love?*
>
> *What do you need more of in our relationship?*
>
> *What are your core needs – the things that you really want to feel?*
>
> *When do you feel most alive and excited in life and about us?*

Then discuss and explore each other's responses and decide to act on them. Give more and don't expect anything in return. This one exercise could change everything.

It Is All About Being Different – Polar Energy

Men and woman are literally polar opposites, not only in their physical make up but in their life energy, purpose and emotional presence. That is what makes us so attracted to each other in a sexual and emotional way. To simplify this further I want to define these differences as polar energies that, when they are opposite, create *polarity*. In the same way you may be familiar with Yin and Yang, polarity between couples can be split into *masculine* energy and *feminine* energy. Conventionally people may refer to this as *man* and *woman*; however, there is masculine and feminine energy in both sexes. Hence, the philosophy can apply to both heterosexual and non-heterosexual couples.

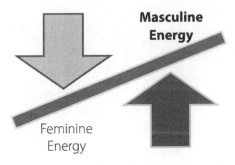

So polarity is like the opposites of a magnet, the dynamic is like a beautifully executed Latin dance – each person pulling and pushing in harmony, dancing with, and around each other in a mesmerising way. This polarity creates sparks, ignites flames and allows the passion to flow between two people. When partners are in their true core energy, either *masculine* or *feminine*, that is when complete polarity exists between them. This is when they feel most connected in a physical and emotional way.

The opposite of polarity is to be de-polarised; this is where a couple's core essence, their masculine and feminine energy, has ebbed away or been eroded. You will see this when you meet couples who describe that they *'have lost something in the relationship'* and that *'It is not like it used to be when we first met.'* When this happens, non-intimate habits form, the dance becomes lifeless, daily routines take over and the couple loses interest in each other at a deeper, more intimate level. They slowly become just friends sharing the same environment or home. They operate like flat-mates.

It is clear that the first essential ingredient to attracting an amazing partner into your life and for creating a successful, loving, passionate and long-lasting relationship is to establish and continue to maintain polarity between each other.

Polarity – It's OK To Be Different

The underlying message here is that you and your partner need to accept that you are different and that is what creates the polarity dynamic. If you both become the same energy and person you will not only morph into one entity, but you will literally become the same energy. I have seen it where the man becomes more feminine in his core and the woman creates a hardened shell of masculine presence so that they almost appear to be the same person. Equally, in some relationships, a battle of values emerges; for example, one person wanting more adventure and fun whilst the other wants more security and comfort. The wedge starts to form and one tries to force their values on the other.

This does not work, so my message is simply this – accept each other for who you are and then start to work on growing both individually and together. As I describe the feminine and masculine energy in the next section I would like you to be a silent witness. Ask yourself how this knowledge of your partner's energy could help you meet their needs and desires. Understanding the difference plays a huge role in making your relationship amazing.

Feminine Energy Flows

Feminine energy is a flowing, radiant and life-creating energy that moves in alignment with the earth, the sun and oceans. This is an energy that should not be contained or controlled, by its very nature it has no specific direction, it simply flows in a beautiful and playful way. Feminine energy comes from within and then becomes expressed on the outside. For example, when a woman is in her true feminine core this energy shows up in how she looks, dresses and behaves on the outside.

Remember also that both men and women have feminine energy within them. In some men this energy is more prevalent than others. Equally, when a woman is in her true feminine flow she radiates attraction to those around her. The feminine energy inside her likes to feel loved, to feel attractive, noticed and desired. It is this wild, uncontrolled open energy that attracts, for example, men with a strong masculine core.

You can really tell when a woman is in her feminine flow because no matter what is going on around her, if she sees something beautiful like a rose, a child playing or a lovely piece of clothing she will be drawn to it. Men may see this as being distracted and non-focused, but actually she is in her flow – going with the moment and enjoying beauty. She can mentally and emotionally move between different things that are in her world quite effortlessly.

The feminine energy has a massive attraction to masculine energy. No matter what the sex of the person, the core energy is what drives the attraction. Hence masculine and feminine energy can exist as an attractive force in both heterosexual and non-heterosexual couples. In the case of a woman in her true feminine she will generally be less attracted to a man who is more feminine than masculine – her core energy is drawn to the masculine energy in the man she is seeking. This is something that a lot of guys today do not understand.

Masculine Energy Focuses

Masculine energy is a physical, purpose and focus-driven energy that likes to experience completion in a single-minded way. Masculine energy resides within both men and women and like feminine energy it can be stronger in either. However, biologically, masculine energy tends to be stronger in men. Masculine energy is not about size, bulk and physical presence – we are talking about calm, centred masculine core energy that breaks through when faced with a challenge, that does not back down when pushed against and that has a single-minded purpose. In essence masculine energy is mission-driven and focused.

Masculine men generally have a clear direction about where they are going in life and ooze a quiet confidence. He will have a strong purpose or mission to his life and this will often be the focus of his activities. The masculine core tends to focus on one thing at a time, be it work, sport, relationship, sexual release, creating wealth – it is usually one thing at a time. The one thing that can distract a masculine man from his focus is a strong feminine force that is so attractive to him that he cannot ignore it. If his partner, for example, walks up to him when he is trying to work and she is in her true feminine flow, loving and open, he will likely be distracted – at least for a short period!

The masculine energy thrives on challenge, living on the edge and is instinctively protective towards feminine energy. Men who are living in their core masculine energy like adventure, challenge, risk and anything that allows them to stand strong and become the shelter in the storm. It is an innate feeling that sits in the heart of a masculine man. What is most attractive to a feminine woman is the sheer certainty and calmness that a man with strong masculine energy exudes.

Polarity Reversal

These two core energies are essential for creating and maintaining a dynamic, passionate and loving relationship. I have friends and clients who are in passionate non-heterosexual relationships. The dynamic is exactly the same. In the case of two men or women in a relationship, one will generally have a more masculine core energy whilst the other has a stronger feminine energy. This creates the same wonderful attractive forces, passion, intimacy, love and excitement.

In a heterosexual relationship, where I believe problems occur is when a couple start off in their relationship in their natural masculine and feminine cores but over time these switch. The woman goes through changes in her relationship and maybe her career. She starts to develop masculine layers around her that dull and dampen her natural radiant feminine energy. What I mean here is that she becomes more 'to-do list' driven, more focused on achieving business and work-related goal. She feels she has to perform in a similar manner to her male peers at work and the flow that once radiated from her starts to take the masculine form. This becomes magnified if the partner she is with is not his masculine core and so she subconsciously takes on that role. The key is to talk to each other in an open way that allows your core energy to flow.

Janet's Story – The Mum Who Was a Dad Too

In the spring of 2008 I worked with a lady called Janet who approached me about the fact that every time she met a guy and started a relationship, it seemed to end within four or five months. Janet was actually a mother of two lovely children who were 7 and 10 years of age and both of whom lived with her. Her husband had died not long after their second child had been born. Janet was in her late thirties, healthy looking, attractive and had quite a serious demeanour.

Over a few sessions, Janet revealed that after her husband had died she just 'buckled down and took on the role of both mum and dad.' She had become very practical minded, always fixing things, even the plumbing in the house and the kids' bicycles. She had taken on an additional part-time job in the last five years and had not really pampered or treated herself to anything for years. The more she spoke the clearer it became that over this time, Janet's feminine energy had been replaced with a masculine, purpose-driven and functional energy. The way she spoke, walked and held herself was very masculine. In the process of looking after the kids, she had lost touch with her feminine essence. This was the reason her relationships were not working, the men she was attracting were actually not connecting with her, or they were slightly feminine in their energy. What was clear to me was that she really wanted to be with a man that had a stronger masculine energy than hers and who had the courage and care to bring her out of herself again so that she could allow her feminine energy to flow again.

As I explained this to her she literally broke into tears as though a massive pressure had been released. Through this letting go, we explored what she loved about being a woman, and as she spoke she literally transformed. She laughed, touched her hair, stood with her hands on her hips and shifted back into her feminine energy. Over the next few months we worked on this and the old radiant Janet emerged in a beautiful way.

A Message To The Masculine

For simplicity I will refer to the masculine energy in this section as the male energy. If you want to attract an amazing partner and create a passionate, loving and intimate relationship with your partner then I would like to offer you some powerful masculine mantras. These are mantras for anyone whose core energy lies in the masculine. These are statements, declarations, mantras that state who you are and what you want. These must be used in association with the values, conditions and beliefs process that you have applied to the relationship area of your life. As with everything in this book, the first step is to apply my suggestions and see what works. The things that work, keep doing them and the things that don't – try a different approach.

Mantra 1: I am 100% present and I honour my word – for most guys this is very difficult. This is a vital ingredient to having an amazing relationship. What I mean by being 100% present is don't pick up your mobile phone and look at it when talking to you partner; don't look at other distractions, especially other women when talking to her; when in the heat of an argument or discussion, don't walk away, stay with her and see it through. If you promise to do something – do it. This includes even the smallest thing like buying a loaf of bread on the way home from work. When promises get broken on a regular basis, your partner will lose trust in you. If she loses trust one area that gets affected is the intimacy between you. She will not be able to open and be vulnerable at an intimate level if she cannot trust you. You must listen with your ears and your heart. True masculine energy is focused and present.

Mantra 2: *I am decisive and on purpose* – feminine energy is hugely attracted to decisive, purposeful energy. One of the reasons so many male movie stars are admired on screen is because of the decisive, purposeful way they are portrayed. Don't force her to make decisions – you do it. Have a purpose to your life and let her know what it is and that she is part of that. It is this purpose that helps fuel the masculine core inside you. Allow this decisiveness to express through your daily actions and your physiology – the way you walk, talk and act.

Mantra 3: *I am a rock and I love to challenge myself* – when things get difficult, when the world around you both seems to be falling apart or something bad has happened, that's when you step up. You have a warm, open heart and at the same time you are the rock that nothing can break. You are the protector. Your feminine partner needs to know you are there so that she/he can remain in her feminine energy whilst you provide the direction and the protection. Challenge yourself, live on the edge, climb a mountain, sky dive, go on an adventure, push yourself beyond your comfort zone – this will continue to stimulate the natural masculine energy within you.

Mantra 4: *I am committed to my beautiful partner* – This means all of the first mantra and much more must be practiced every day. This does not mean flying off on different projects all over the country and the world all the time – leaving your partner regularly, creating distance between you and then expecting that when you get back things will be fine. Feminine energy needs commitment and presence. So act committed, give more of yourself each day, love unconditionally and look to meet your partner's primary needs/values on a regular basis.

Putting Words Into Action

To develop your masculine energy and to help connect and create polarity with your feminine partner there are several things that you can do on a daily and practical basis. You can take up a sport that stretches you physically, try something that puts you to the test like a parachute jump or climbing a mountain, get out into the wild and connect with nature, hook up with other masculine men who are in their core, work out, try a new adventure or try a new business venture. To connect with your partner, surprise them with a romantic experience, treat them to wild and passionate experience, be present when you are with her. If you have children, take them out for a day and treat her to a day at the spa. Be the rock, the shelter and the one that protects your family.

A Message to The Feminine

For simplicity I will refer to the feminine energy in this section as the female energy. I am speaking here as a man about feminine energy and I will share with you my insights and those of my beautiful Stine (my fiancée) who has an amazing understanding of the feminine core. Here are three feminine mantras for you to practice if your core energy is feminine (female energy).

Mantra 1: *I live in my heart and stay open to love* – this is a powerful reminder of the core essence of feminine energy and when her heart is open she will give herself totally. I have personally witnessed female friends that have lost their feminine shine by being in their heads most of the time. They have been hurt by a relationship that went wrong and so they have created a shell around their heart that has closed. So remind yourself that you are a glowing, overflowing heart that spreads love everywhere you go. That is part of the amazing attraction of the feminine – its capacity to love in all circumstances. Life, work and circumstances can drive a woman into her head and out of her heart. Your heart is the source of your feminine energy and so this is where you must flow from every day. When you do this, you will attract the masculine energy that you are seeking. If you are in a partnership, this love will serve to complete their masculine core.

Mantra 2: *I radiate feminine energy* – This is an incredibly attractive force, this is the external emission of what is inside you. Allow yourself to dress in a feminine way, pamper yourself, laugh, dance, be carefree and sing out loud. If your radiant feminine energy becomes dull and loses its shine, you will start to die inside. You will start to notice a shift in the polarity between you and your partner. It is this radiant energy that your partner loves – the masculine cannot resist this amazingly sexy and appealing presence.

Mantra 3: *I stay in my feminine and let him stay in his masculine* – This may sound odd, but is happens more and more in this modern, results and material-driven society. In heterosexual relationships for example, it is important that you as the woman, allow him to stay in his masculine flow. If you allow your true feminine energy to flow, he can feel secure in the knowledge that he can protect, be a rock, step up when he needs to and be there for you. Try it. Remember this is not about who is right or wrong.

Putting Words Into Action

To nurture this amazing feminine energy that is abundant inside you and to connect and stimulate your relationship, there are many different things that you can do on a daily basis which can include going for a massage, dance, meditate, a candlelit bath, do some hands-on charity work, helping others, nurturing your family and your children, make love in the day with your partner, dress up in sexy clothing, pamper your partner, allow your partner to make love to you in a wild and unusual place, get together with other feminine friends to just flow and simply allow time to enjoy the beauty of a walk in the sun. There are many other ways to connect with your core energy. The important thing is to be open to change and to go with your natural flow.

Attracting and Keeping Your Soul Mate

Is it possible I hear you ask and if it is how do I keep the passion and excitement going? Well the answer to the first part of the question is unequivocally yes and to the second part of the question is to go back and apply what I have shared in the rest of this chapter. So let me finish this chapter with what I believe to be a beautiful and natural way to attract, develop and nurture an amazing partner into your life and to sustain a passionate and inspiring relationship.

Know what you want and become the person you want to attract – everything we have covered in this book becomes a vital ingredient here. If you are whole as a person and you have clear empowering beliefs, pure uplifting values and a strong sense of purpose, then you will create a much more attractive energy to those around you. It is essential that you are clear on what your top two or three Core Values are. Go back to the chapter on values if you need more clarity. If you do not know your Core Values you will not be able to check how well they align with your potential partner.

Be authentic – be yourself – when I met Stine, my fiancée, I was very open with her about my circumstances and my life. There is an age difference between us of 14 years and when we met I was going through a serious period of change in my life, some of which was not good. I was open about this and with that level of honesty and sense of who I was, I was able to create a strong connection with her. Only when you are completely yourself will you be able to connect with the values, beliefs, passions and chemistry of the person you are dating. This will enable you to connect with the real nature of that person. This also means staying in your core energy be it masculine or feminine.

Establish their top Core Values (needs) and satisfy those needs – this is an essential ingredient without which most relationships would fail rapidly. If you can become a master of reading your partner's needs and giving unconditionally to help meet those needs, then they will love being with and around you. Imagine if the two of you were focused on meeting each other's needs and creating polarity, passion and excitement even in the smallest things that you do – what an amazing relationship that would be. For example, if your partner has a Core Value of excitement and fun, then create opportunities for them to experience this – book a surprise trip abroad, a party, a theatre trip or even a bungee jump.

It Takes Effort But It's Worth It

My final message is to say that in any great relationship there are ups and downs. That is the nature of polarity and the dynamics of two people engaging at an intimate level every day. Yes it takes work and yes it takes effort – but this effort can be graceful and fun. It will mean doing things when you are tired and drained from your other activities. It will mean giving up some temporary gratification elsewhere to stay committed to the relationship. Don't give up. Don't point the finger or lay blame. Take responsibility for giving more to the relationship each day and don't trade your efforts or love for something in the relationship. Just love unconditionally and enjoy the journey.

12 | **Money** - Manage Your Finances and Create Wealth

Introduction

The subject of money, security and wealth is simply something that I could not leave out of this book. From all my experiences and observations, most people encounter challenges in this area at some point in their lives. In fact, it is broadly quoted that money is the biggest cause of relationship and marital break-ups. I have been privileged to have helped thousands of people on the path to financial freedom and would like to share some of the insights I have learnt during this journey.

In this chapter I will take you very quickly into the mind of the wealthiest people in the world. Why? Because no matter what your current circumstances are, the greatest change in your situation will come from studying and copying the strategies and beliefs that they have. Higher earnings, abundance, getting out of debt and financial security will ONLY come when you grow from the inside – not the other way around.

The way you react and engage in this chapter will vary dramatically depending on your relationship with money. You may be in a very dark place financially right now where you are possibly even experiencing bankruptcy. If that is the case, then your perception will likely be one that associates pain with money. On the other hand, you may be financially very comfortable and have a relatively healthy relationship with money. In which case you can use these tools to enhance your position and help others do the same. Either way, I would like you to embrace the concepts and teachings that I present to you in this chapter. The details of these teachings will be the subject of a future book.

Since I started developing my wealth through property investing around 2001 – 2002, I have also been privileged to teach and speak in front of audiences around the world on this very subject. I have encountered people with virtually every possible belief and relationship to money. I have even had members of the audience who were homeless and in order to raise the money to pay for the seminar they had been begging on the streets. Now that is what I call a desire to learn and grow.

Your Financial Template

In the early chapters of this book we discussed your self-communication, beliefs, Core Values and your environment past and present. You will recall that we also discussed the seven blocks that can stop you making positive change. All of these characteristics and factors combine together to create a template for how you live your life. The word 'template' is defined as a form, a mould, or a pattern used as a guide to making something. As a young engineer I used templates for technical drawings – the template enabled me to use a pen to create the same image in my drawing every time. The only way to create a different result was to change or modify the template.

We can use the analogy of templates and apply it to every part of our lives. You will have a template for your health, your relationships, how you communicate and without doubt a template for how you deal with your finances and money. We will call this your financial template. This financial template defines everything that you experience that is related to your finances and includes:

+ *Your spending and saving habits*
+ *Your choice of income generation e.g. job, self-employed, entrepreneur*
+ *Your risk profile to money*
+ *The type of investments that you do or do not make*
+ *The ability or inability to deal with debt*
+ *How well you manage your finances*

Even one single limiting belief relating to money can have a massive knock-on effect in any of the above areas. Imagine going through your life struggling financially and never being able to double or triple your income because of one belief or a set of value conditions that are not serving you properly. That would be a tragedy of Shakespearean proportions – a lifelong struggle that can easily be avoided with some personal growth. The truth is that this situation probably happens to over 90% of the population.

Sometimes I meet people who literally beat themselves up over how they have got themselves into financial trouble. Please don't do this to yourself. Remember that your financial template is forged from the experiences, observations and beliefs that were imparted upon you by other people at an early age. What's done is done and it is now time to address any issues, take responsibility and move forward.

The biggest influence on your financial template, more than anything else, is likely to have been your parents, immediate family and/or money-related significant emotional events that have occurred in the past. Let me give you an example.

Sahira's Story

Sahira was another client of mine who was originally born overseas and moved over to the UK when she was 5 years of age. When I first met her she was quiet in nature, warm and caring and a very smart person with a real love for her family. Although

Sahira was in a fairly good job, she came to me to deal with a growing realization that she truly wanted more from her life on a financial and personal level. She was clear that it was time to change and had a great sense of urgency because she'd been stuck doing the same thing but could not figure out what her block was. I loved her passion and commitment and I quickly realized that this was a financial template issue.

To cut a long story short, when she was around 4 years of age Sahira's father died, leaving Sahira, her brother and her mum with the large business and several assets. The family was financially secure for life. Then, like a bolt of lightning, her uncle (her father's brother) stepped in and took everything. In her words, he "stole all their money". Sahira, her mum and her brother were turned out onto the street and became homeless. This led to a long and painful journey bringing them all the way to the UK.

Once in the United Kingdom, her mother took on menial jobs and worked every available hour to keep the family afloat. However, over the next 30 years her mother never did any more than was necessary to survive because she believed that any money that she had spare would be taken from her again.

Just like her mother, Sahira's financial template had also been shaped by this painful experience. She did work hard and tried to put some money aside in the hope that she could break the pattern. However, two more significant events occurred. Firstly her father's family came to the UK on a visit and demanded that she give them what little money she had put aside, which she did. Then she met a guy and got married and in a short space of time, her husband's family stepped in and also took whatever money she had left.

So by the time I met Sahira she had a financial template that had some incredibly strong negative beliefs about money and creating wealth. She was literally locked in a mental box that stopped her taking any chances or trying any new opportunities in case she made money and then had it taken from her. This was why she had never stretched beyond her circumstances, never pushed herself for promotion or started her own business.

Not everybody experiences situations as extreme as Sahira's, however, I believe that her story clearly illustrates how certain events in our past can shape our attitude, beliefs and rules around money.

If you wish to develop a healthier relationship with money and attract more wealth into your life then it is vital that you journey back in time to identify any possible areas where a small or more significant event may have shaped a negative belief for you. In some cases it may not need to be a specific experience that happened to you, it might simply be an observation that you made that had a significant impact on you. On the other hand, it may be a series of smaller experiences and negative messages that you heard repeatedly and that have built up over the years. Think of a great oak tree being cut down by someone simply using an axe and chopping again and again until it falls.

People either gravitate towards over-spending their money, or saving like crazy and never trying anything else, or ignoring their financial situation in the hope it will go away or simply feeling that they are too good for money and that there is no need to discuss it or focus on it. Your finances will be reflected directly by which one of these people that you are.

The Consequences of Not Understanding Your Financial Template

I have met tens of thousands of people who have had a desire to improve their financial situation, earn more money, develop property businesses, trade the markets, build a bigger business and ultimately create more security and wealth. Many I have taught, others I have mentored and others I have met at the same seminars that I myself have attended; all of them were hungry to learn and become wealthier in a small or big way. However, just a few years into my journey of growth in this area I was shocked just how few actually achieve their dream. Later, when I started speaking to audiences, this awareness became magnified.

Anyone who visits my website will know that part of my mission on earth is to educate people on the subject of money, security and wealth. My brand *The Bald Truth* grew out of sharing a *direct* message with people, telling them what they needed to hear, not what they wanted to hear. So what I really need to tell you is that the cause of failure for those that were seeking greater wealth was not the 'how to', it was purely their financial template. This template had been moulded in such a way that no matter what they tried to do, the old patterns repeated themselves each time because the template was not set for wealth creation at an early age. Ignoring this is like committing financial suicide. Worst still, the pattern will repeat again and again.

However your financial template is shaped, it will affect the financial aspects of every area of your life including your work, career, business, investments and personal life. So we need to have a look at it, identify the bad elements that are causing you pain and stopping the flow of money to you and then we remove these and redesign the template for wealth-building.

What Did You See and Hear About Money?

Over the past 20 years of working with people I have learnt to ask specific questions that get right to heart of the issue, whether it be health, love, money, career – whatever. When it comes to money, there are several questions that I like to ask in order to identify any areas of pain or negative associations with money. The more that you dig, the more open your subconscious mind will become to remembering even the smallest things. Here are some typical questions. The term 'parents' in this situation also related to people that you were very close to in your younger years:

What are the typical things you heard your parents say about their finances?

What were your parents' beliefs about how to handle the finances?

Did you observe any arguments about money?

What did your parents say about rich people?

What events occurred that caused some level of pain in relation to money and finances?

There are many other questions that can be asked and the important thing as you go through this process is to ask yourself how this made you feel about money. What beliefs did you develop as a result of this? How has this affected your life financially and the choices you have made?

In some cases observations that you made and the things that you heard would have resulted in a positive impact upon your financial template. In other cases, especially the significant painful events, it will have left you with a negative pattern.

Empowering observations and phrases that you may have observed include:

"You deserve to be wealthy"

"You can earn as much money as you like"

"If you give lots of value you will receive great rewards"

On the other hand, typical negative statements may have included:

"Money does not grow on trees"

"It's all right for rich people, they can afford it, they have it easy"

"We are not like them, they are rich, we're not"

"Money is the root of all evil"

"We can't afford it, so don't even ask"

"Do you think I am made of money?"

Think about the damage these statements can make to your beliefs about your finances. Your whole understanding and beliefs around the subject of money would be based on a sense of lack and jealousy. Remember that the first step to change is awareness. The process you are going through here is raising awareness of your relationship with your finances, money and where these beliefs stem from.

Abundance and Scarcity

If I could simplify the message even further it would be to say the intention from which you approach money can come from one of two places: abundance or scarcity. Another word for scarcity in this situation is fear.

When a person is coming from a place of scarcity or fear then virtually anything they do related to money is about protecting what they have. Scarcity mentality means that you do not want to share with anybody else; you are afraid that other people might take your money or opportunity from you; you focus on protecting or not spending your money first and fundamentally this means that you do not believe there is enough money in the world.

When a person is living life with an abundant mentality, they totally believe that there is a complete abundance of money and wealth in the world. They are happy to share opportunities and inspire others to do the same. They are less guarded about investment opportunities and creating wealth with other people. Actually, they live in a place of love with a healthy respect for money rather than the fear of money. They see financial challenges as an opportunity to learn and develop new skills in managing money.

Change Your Financial Template

Having reached this stage in the book you should be very familiar with the process of redefining beliefs, Core Values and the conditions around each value having done this as part of the Six Step Change Process.

Later in this chapter I will describe the key qualities of wealthy people. You may wish to read that section before completing the following exercise. Allow an evening to work through this without interruptions.

Model Successful People

On a new page in your journal put the title My New Financial Template. Your first subtitle is Wealthy, Financially Successful And Abundant People Who Inspire Me And Who Have Great Financial Templates. Under this heading I would like you to list out any people who you respect who fall into the category of the above heading and who you believe have a strong financial template. This might include people like George Soros, Warren Buffett, Anita Roddick, Lynn Twist, Robert Kiyosaki, Angelina Jolie, Donald Trump, to name just a few. Remembering here that we are not just focusing on material wealth (you can if you wish). However, you may wish to also look at people who also inspire you through their ability to earn, create, contribute to others or raise money for charitable causes.

Copy Their Beliefs

Looking at the names of the people you have written down, now imagine what it would be like to be these people. You may need to close your eyes and picture their lifestyle and how they act on a day-to-day basis. As you start to do this I want you to notice the beliefs, values and the rules that they have. In your journal put another heading Positive Money Beliefs. Now list out all the positive money beliefs that you can imagine these people have. Examples may include 'I am worthy of being a millionaire', 'I attract opportunities to me every day', 'I love money and use it for helping my family and others who are in need', 'I am great at handling and managing my finances' and 'I get paid every day for adding value in my job or business'.

Create New Money Values and Conditions

Finally close your eyes again and ask yourself what Core Values do these people have around money and wealth. As you start to picture these values, then imagine what type of conditions that they have in place in order to achieve these values. Remember you can go back to the previous chapters and remind yourself of this process. Here are a few examples.

Value: Attraction (the feeling of attracting great wealth and money)

Conditions For Experiencing Attraction: 'I feel like I am attracting money by simply talking to other people about what opportunities exist in the world.' 'I know I am attracting wealth, because every day I see new opportunities in property, in my career, in the money markets and in business.'

Value: Financially Responsible (the feeling of being financially responsible)

Conditions For Achieving Financial Responsibility: 'I know I am financially responsible when I value every penny I see or find' or 'I am financially responsible by simply knowing how to monitor my expenses and income.'

Get inspired by this process and you will quickly find that the way you act with money, your job, career and opportunity will dramatically change.

Global Recipe of The Rich
(Rich People Think Differently)

As I have already mentioned previously, one of the most effective ways to change your circumstances and the way you see the world is to study other people who are successful and abundant in the areas you want to grow. In this chapter we are looking at financial intelligence, money and how people manage their money. There is nobody better to study than wealthy people if you want to master these specific areas. I have summarised the characteristics of wealthy people that I personally know, that I practice and have observed in others. But first a little more about my story.

Are You Prepared to Change In Order to Create Wealth?

I grew up in an environment where the philosophy was to get a good education, work hard and earn a good living. My mother, although she had the chance to go to grammar school, did not do so due to financial limitations in her family and her father's belief that she should get a good job. My father earned a Masters in Mechanical Engineering and came to England and worked and died as an engineer. We did not have a lot of money and neither of my parents had been taught or understood the formula for creating wealth. What was inspiring for me was that my mother worked and sacrificed to help me and my brothers get educated and encouraged us to pursue our dreams.

Since my parents were unable to offer me any schooling in wealth creation I had to go out and learn about it. I invested tens of thousands of pounds into wealth education seminars and mentors; I read books and started associating with wealthy people. Most importantly I was open and humble enough to realize I needed to change and was prepared to put in the work behind it. The results were truly inspiring to me. Our lives changed. We purchased around 40 properties in just over a year with virtually no money to start with and continued to expand that business. My lifestyle changed and with it came new, exciting opportunities. In order to operate in this new world I had to change my relationship with money and my beliefs about becoming wealthy.

As my businesses grew, with my new-found success came new challenges like one of my personal friends and business partners going bankrupt and one of my businesses failing. Through these challenges, I became stronger and it forced me to review my financial beliefs, how I approached new opportunities and the way I worked with new partners. Amazingly, as I write this book in the heart of one the toughest recessions in our history, I receive more opportunities for increasing wealth than ever before.

I would like to share with you the *recipe* that we have used and many of the wealthiest people living today use for creating and managing their money. I would suggest you take the time to go and study these, and start to ask 'Where in my life can I immediately apply parts or all of this formula.' Remember that this is not a microwave recipe; you will need to put the ingredients together in the right order, then turn on the heat and bring it to the boil by creating strong initial momentum and then keeping a steady heat to cook it through to achieve your required result:

- ✦ *Have A Clear Vision*

- ✦ *Become A Great Financial Manager*

- ✦ *Focus On The Four Pillars Of Wealth Creation*

- ✦ *Utilize The Incredible Power Of Compounding*

- ✦ *Create Massive Value For Others*

- ✦ *Adapt To All Market Conditions*

- ✦ *Give A Percentage Of Your Earnings To Charity*

You may not want to be rich and have millions in the bank – that is fine. However, fundamentally, if you are reading this book and in-particular this chapter, then you probably want to improve your financial situation or maybe that of others around you. If that is the case, then there is no better source to learn from than wealthy people. The degree of wealth and security that you develop is then your choice – but the principles can be applied to everyone.

Since these wealth ingredients could easily be the subject of a whole book, I have chosen to share two that I believe are essential in the whole context of what I am teaching in this book – Clarity Of Vision and Mastering Your Finances. I would encourage you to attend one of my seminars so that you can explore this subject in greater depth.

Have A Clear Vision

I cannot emphasise the importance of this message. It is a teaching that is often shared from stages around the world, in audio programs, in classrooms, seminars and books, and yet truthfully, the mass of the population still neglect to apply it to their lives.

I am sure you have heard the legendary words of Martin Luther King, "I have a dream…" this was a vision that over time became a reality and changed history. In your darkest hours, the only true way to raise your spirit up and beyond your circumstances is to have a vision bigger and more inspiring than your current reality – a vision for the future. Even in your greatest moments, having a vision of how your life continues to be is inspirational.

Many people find it difficult to have a true vision of wealth that they can believe would be true for themselves. Often they will experience this lifestyle not by actually living it but by following the lives of movie stars or celebrities on TV. They develop a belief that this lifestyle is only for the chosen few and so they switch off dreaming for themselves. They settle for watching others and never create a deep-rooted belief that it is something they can have if they are prepared to change and put the work in to make it happen.

In Chapter 9 we explored in detail the importance of creating clarity of vision and purpose and I would recommend that you revisit that chapter and apply the principles to creating a financial vision for your future.

Become A Master Of Your Finances

People who have built their fortunes have done so through (1) creating wealth and (2) managing it well. In fact, if a person cannot respect and manage £1 then they will struggle to manage £10 or £100 and therefore they will never be able to manage £1,000,000. It is as simple as that. Rich people understand the need to control where they allocate the wealth that they have created. We learnt this quickly as we started to build our businesses and property portfolio.

You may have personally experienced being in a situation where you have earned more money one year, made more cash on a deal or a business, maybe had a bonus or a windfall. Then a year or so later you find yourself asking, 'Where has all that money gone?' or 'Why is it I can work so hard and yet still not appear to have as much as I had hoped?' Does that sound familiar? If so, then it is likely that your existing system for managing your finances is not working.

Brian And Susan – Living It Up

In 2007 I was speaking at a seminar in London on the importance of tracking your income and expenses in order to be able to help your money movement and create a clearer picture of how you can put more money aside for building wealth. In the coffee break a lovely couple approached me who were probably in their early 40s. They shared with me that they both were working in careers that paid quite well. I recall they were bringing into the household just around £40,000 each and had no children. From what they said to me, they had recently come to a strong realization that they really wanted to start a family but felt frustrated that they 'did not seem to have any money left after each month.'

They were excited by what I had been showing with my slides, assessing Income vs Outgoings and then creating a system of accounts to allocate spare funds. They said that in the 9 years that they had been married, they had never monitored their expenses. I asked, "How do you know how much residual (spare) cash you have at the end of each month to put aside?"

They laughed and said, "That's why we are so excited – we don't know and never have done – we have simply been living it up." Their approach had been to check the account about a week before the end of each month to ensure it was not below zero. If it was above zero, then they would spend the last bit on gadgets, meals, 'things', in order to reduce the account down to zero.

In their words, "We had no vision or purpose for our money beyond having fun, so that's all we did, just spent our money on having fun. Now we want a family and to help our future children. Now we can see that we have a different purpose." They were a smart couple and by the end of the day they worked out that they could reduce their outgoings to such an extent that they could put about £2400 per month into an investment vehicle that would grow and still enable them to have fun and start a family. That is why they were excited. Simply having a money allocation system in place could allow them to start to create wealth.

In the case of most of the people I have worked with, it was not until we gained clarity on how to manage their finances properly that we were able to establish a specific path forward. Every single penny you earn must have a purpose, it may sound extreme but without this foundation principle in place you will literally find yourself bleeding cash every month. If you ask any of the clients that I personally mentored they will tell you this is an area of revelation when we talk about money. The laws of wealth start with the understanding that money is simply energy and that in order for this energy to flow it must be given a purpose. So let's put this ethos into a practical framework.

Many years ago I read a great book called *The Richest Man In Babylon* by George S. Clason. In this book he talked about the principle of taking a percentage of your earnings and putting it into your wealth-building vehicle. I have since studied and experimented with many different models allocating the money that I earn, all of which follow a similar theme, but produce a positive result. The finance allocation approach below is one that works well. You will need to work with it as a template and you can choose to refine it based on your own circumstances. The critical thing is that you have some kind of system in place that is automated and creates a set of spending and investing rules for you to follow.

If you are currently in debt and have financial challenges going on right now, then the allocation of your finances we are going to cover is essential for you. Irrespective of how much you are currently earning the essential thing that you MUST do is break your existing pattern of spending and financial management. For you to be in financial trouble must mean that what you are doing does not work. The approach I will share with you does work when applied consistently over time. You will still need to address your debts and their repayment, but at least with the system to follow, you will be able to balance that with other financial allocations.

**Since I am not a financial advisor I must remind you that the principles I share should not be taken as advice – they are simply systems that I and other wealthy people implement. If you are uncertain on any aspect of your finances you should seek the advice of a professional independent financial adviser.

Allocation of Personal Finances

The first thing is to separate your main bank account (personal) from any other business or related accounts. This is a common mistake and it can cause confusion. Whether you are employed, in a job, on a pension or in business, my experience has been that a clean and clear separate account is an essential starting point. So the starting point is to have all household income coming into one main account.

From this one account you will pay money out into key areas of your life.

Yes you can expand on this and add additional accounts that allow the development of other areas of your life, but for now keep it simple. Unfortunately, the average person tends to spend in accordance with where their greatest pain or greatest pleasure is focused. That means that their earnings follow no system. One month it may be a new flat screen TV (Fun spending) and the next month they may be dealing with a late payment on a credit card (Debt spending), then another month taking money from savings to pay for a deposit on a new car or a motorbike (Fun spending) rather than long-term wealth (Wealth investing). Get the picture? No plan, no financial allocation system and no wealth strategy.

The model illustrated above prevents this from happening because you start every month with a set amount of money allocated into each of these accounts.

Look again at the diagram above. The principle here is that we all need to cover our basic living expenses (Living Account) and separate to this we may have loans and credit cards to pay off (Debt Account). If you have no debts then there is no money transferred into this account. Instead you re-allocate the funds into other accounts of your choice. In order to build wealth we must also allocate a certain amount every month to an investment vehicle (Wealth Account). At my seminars and on my website I spend time explaining what vehicles people can use to accelerate their wealth. These funds could potentially be used in such vehicles. The area that usually is an issue for people who never develop wealth is spending or Fun money. This is usually an area of overspend. However, it is essential that if you are earning money that you reward and treat yourself – so you must have fun (Fun Account).

The last area that many people put off 'until I make more money' is charity and contribution (Charity Account). Tithing is a principle practiced by millions around the world. My experience and observation of most modern-thinking wealthy people is that they understand that no matter what level you earn at, when you are open to giving even a small percentage of what you earn then you are open to receiving more money. Wealthy people give and understand this basic law. Poor people often don't give – they wait to make more money. But sadly, they rarely get there because they don't understand that this giving to others is an essential rule of becoming wealthy.

Follow the system and give it a chance to work for you. This means sticking to it and allowing at least six months for it to create momentum and for you to notice the impact. No matter how low or high an earner you are – the same system can be applied to any income.

A Summary to Get Started

In order to really break this down I normally have to look at each person's individual circumstances to provide a more accurate guideline on getting this system to work. However, I would like to give you a starting point.

It is up to you how you set this up. We use different bank accounts and have much of it automated through what are called standing orders. The following breakdown will need to be adjusted according to your circumstances and I am simply giving you a range to operate within. Each of these is a percentage of the net income that arrives in your bank account after being taxed. If you are self-employed or run a business then it helps to use a set monthly amount that you draw from your business and apply the percentages to that. Naturally, if we were sitting one-to-one, I would be asking you about your long-term vision and wealth and security goals. Having established these we would then specify fixed percentages for each area. For example, someone wanting to build a long-term pot of money would reduce their living costs, fun and spending and increase the investment percentage.

Account	% of Net Income	Comment
Living Costs	40 - 60	*Basic living costs*
Fun/Social - non essentials	5 - 15	*Spend on what you like*
Charity - Tithing	5 - 10	*Giving to a cause*
Debt Repayment	0 - 15	*Paying off debt*
Investments - Savings	5 - 30+	*Wealth-building vehicles*
Total	**100%**	**Total must not exceed 100%**

The total of all the percentages must always add up to 100%. All you need to do is choose the appropriate apportions for your current lifestyle. Here are a few examples.

Example 1: Let's say that you don't have any debt, you have low living costs and you are highly focused on building your wealth faster. Then you might choose the following allocation:

Living Costs (45%), Fun (10%), Charity (5%), Debt (0%) and Investments (40%)

Example 2: If you are currently holding debt that requires you to pay at least £295 per month, for example, and you have higher living costs, then your allocation system may be as follows:

Living Costs (60%), Fun (5%), Charity (5%), Debt (20%) and Investments (10%) = 100%

As you become more organized it is vital to work closely to these approximate figures to enable your system to have a positive impact. Avoid varying this every month. It is important to have a plan, a percentage for each area and stick to it. Personally, my view is that the Wealth Account should be compromised as little as possible. Learn to always put money into this account no matter how challenging things are. When there are spare funds available this is a great account to add more to.

Final Comment

What I have covered here is a fantastic foundation for you to build
on. Financial intelligence can be learnt and developed. It would
be a pleasure to see you at one of my personal development and
wealth creation seminars. In this arena you will really get to work
at a deeper level on this and many other areas. The important thing
in this whole process is to stay relaxed, enjoy it and don't allow
tension to creep in. Dealing with money should be fun – that way
you create a healthy relationship with abundance and the flow of
money that comes to you.

Where The Rubber Meets The Road

13 Are You Ready To Make It Happen?

Introduction

You have either arrived at this page because you wanted to flick to the back to see what suggestions I make in concluding the book and guiding you forward or you have followed me on the whole journey through this book and you have now come to the end. If you are the first person, then feel free to look over this chapter and I recommend that you dive into the chapters that you believe will help you make the necessary changes in your life right now.

If you are the second person then *CONGRATULATIONS* – we have come on a long journey together. We covered a huge amount of insights and knowledge in just one book. It now comes down to three things: your desire to change, your commitment to change and your belief that you deserve to live a more inspiring and fulfilling life. They all work together and like cogs in an engine, if one does not turn, it stops the others working too.

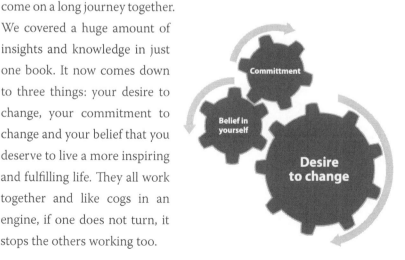

Desire to Change

Having come this far, trust me when I say that you do have the desire to change, one hundred percent. You would not have come this far without the desire. Your desire to change may well be driven by a high level of pain. We often take bigger action and become more driven when we experience greater pain and that is fine; however, the key is to also give that momentum a specific direction otherwise it will have been wasted effort. You will be like a sprinter who runs 50 metres and then runs out of track and does not know where to go next. That is where your purpose and vision come into play. So it is important to also move towards what you truly, passionately want to attract into your life.

You Deserve to Have an Amazing Life

Let's be brutally honest, if things are not right for you at this moment in your life and you are unhappy with something, then you can either choose to live a pretty unhappy existence, living emotionally in a dark place, never truly being happy and bordering on depression; or you can lead a mediocre life, getting by, keeping the same job or business and doing enough to cover the bills and have a few vacations now and then, have average health and you can survive; or you can live a full and inspiring life, doing what you are passionate about, pursuing different projects, having great health and vitality together with a loving, intimate relationship and have money, security and be able to help others along the way.

The choice is yours!

That is what's so exciting, you simply have to believe it and it will become true to you. Once it becomes true to you then you will start to act accordingly. That is what the essence of this book has been about – giving you the tools to redefine those beliefs, values and rules to CREATE the life changes and the life that you deserve. It is your birthright as a human being to be able to nurture all the amazing gifts you were given on the day you were born. You deserve to be who you want to be – not who others want you to be or who you think they want you to be.

How Committed Are You?

Reading a book is one thing; taking regular and consistent action on what you have learnt is another. You only have to look at the thousands of people who join fitness gyms across the world, learn the basic exercises and then stop going to the gym. In truth, the same applies to the personal development and self-help industry.

All I can suggest is this – be different to the average person. Give yourself the gift of applying some or all of the methods I have shared for at least three months and one day. Not 10 days or 21 days or even 60 days – give yourself at least a quarter of a year and one day.

Why this time period? Simple, you can start developing a habit in under a month. You start with small steps doing daily activities based on the exercises we have covered. This breaks the inertia that you may have been experiencing. But that is not enough. After 10 days you will have picked up momentum but could be distracted. After 21 to 30 days, typically, the good habits and beliefs are starting to become part of your thinking. However, what I have observed in others and myself is that these new changes are still in their infancy after 30 days.

In the mentoring that I do with clients I have observed that over a three-month period of accountability and by checking in on core beliefs, values, rules and habits – the clients make a noticeable shift from the start-up phase to the continued momentum phase. It is much harder to stop a train once it has created momentum. That is why you need at least three months.

Your commitment to changing your circumstances, who you are and how you show up in the world will be in direct proportion to the clarity you have of your vision, purpose and desire to change. Revisit the chapter on Vision and Purpose if you need more clarity in this area.

Daily Gratitude

My father was a Buddhist and one of the messages I can still remember that he left with me before he died was the importance of practicing gratitude for the things we have in our lives. Since my father's passing I have been blessed with many great mentors and inspirational people, who have touched my life in countless ways. Every one of these people, without exception, has shared the same belief that being grateful for even the smallest blessings that we experience is essential to our emotional, financial and spiritual growth.

We live in what I call a microwave world these days, people seem to want things instantly and become frustrated when their desires do not materialise quickly enough. I know because I have been there. When we manifest frustration about the things that are not occurring for us, we create negative and low vibrational energy at a cellular level in our body. This has been proven on hundreds of thousands of people through kinesiology (muscle testing). Living in a place of frustration for what we don't have also reflects an innate lack of gratitude for what we do have. This in turn, I believe, leads to the attraction of more frustration, low energy and negative circumstances. In other words, people who live in a frustrated way, without gratitude, become more frustrated day by day.

Having come so far in this book I would like to encourage you to experience a new and inspirational habit – daily gratitude. This simply involves taking 10 to 15 minutes each day to close your eyes and to focus on, and feel at a deeper level, the things in your life for which you are grateful. It is also powerful to record these in your journal. It can be anything. Gratitude for an event that happened in your life, a friendship, memories that make you smile, your children, your family. It could be gratitude for your health or the good fortune of a friend. There is beauty and gratitude in anything we do, from a simple smile to the petals of a rose opening in the morning sun. I am grateful to be able to share these words with you.

When you are in this place in your heart, your head is able to move aside and allow the flow of great things to occur. Breathe deeply and slowly and notice how you relax more when you are experiencing gratitude. Your heart rate will change, your aura glows and you naturally smile. Your whole emotional and spiritual presence will open and be ready to receive more of what you are grateful for. And you will see the world in a different way. Living with gratitude, means living in love with who you are and the world around you.

So what do you do next?

This is usually the part of the book where the author gives pages of action steps in the hope that the reader will read every one and apply them diligently. I think you have already come along way if you have applied even a third of what I have covered in this book. So I don't want to write pages of actions for you. I do, however, want to give you an outline of how to approach this moving forward. This is the sequence I would suggest you follow, but ultimately the choice is yours:

1. Get some help. We have not discussed this in detail; however, I live with the belief that the most impactful growth can only come from experience and learning from others who are experienced and specialised. Invest in yourself – just do it. I often say to my audiences do not negotiate the cost of your future. Learning is an investment and a much cheaper one than the cost of staying in the same place for years or making big mistakes. Get a mentor or a coach and attend personal growth-type seminars. Feel free to visit my site and look at the types of things that are available in terms of learning and coaching: **www.rohanlive.com** The important thing is to find someone you relate to, who you trust and who inspires you. Then go for it.

2. Quickly recap on the three ingredients that enable positive change (Chapter 1) and the seven blocks that crush positive change (Chapter 2).

3. Then start with your vision which means reviewing Chapter 9 first. This will immediately shift your focus from the things that are weighing you down so that you can breathe and look ahead.

4. Pick one area that you want to work on first – one only. Then work through every element of the Six Step Change Process (Chapters 4 to 9). Aim to get small and rapid results that you can then build on.

5. Take a good look at your environment (Chapter 8). Put new people around you who are uplifting. Attend seminars where you can meet a whole network of positive people.

6. Experience one new activity every two weeks for the next three months – anything. It could be starting Salsa dancing or pole dancing as one of my clients did. It could be travelling to work on a different route, eating different foods, mixing with different people. The point here is to make change a habit.

7. Review and be a silent witness of the things you do. Adjust your approach and take regular action. It does not have to be big things – it just has to be something that moves you forward. Don't get hung up about little things.

8. Log your progress, your emotions and successes in your journal. Take 20 to 30 minutes a day to calmly reflect on what is great in your life, to be grateful for all that you have and to fill up with love from the universe and world around you.

It's Now Up To You

The next steps are yours. I am here for you in spirit and intention. You have all the resources inside you. Make your life inspiring and remember to share your gifts along the way. Ultimately we are all connected energetically. So you can, if you choose, allow yourself to connect with the energy that I have put into writing this book, my intention and desire to help inspire and support you. Just that alone will provide you an additional source of spirit and passion.

I very much hope that I will meet you at some point in the future, maybe at one of my seminars. I would love to hear about the changes that take place as a result of reading this book, or applying some of the tools that I have shared with you. Please feel free to pass your message, testimonial or enquiry through the contact page on my website or email **enquiries@rohanlive.com**

Enjoy the journey. Namaste.

Recommended Reading

As part of my journey I have learnt from some inspiring leaders and teachers in the world of business, spiritual and personal development. I would like to personally thank each of them. One of the best ways I can recognise them here in the pages of this book is to recommend their books and teachings to you. I hope you enjoy these books as much as I have.

Dyer, Dr. Wayne W. *The Power of Intention: Change the way you look at things and the things you look at will change.* Hay House, Inc. 2004

Chopra, Dr Deepak. *Synchrodestiny: Harnessing the Infinite Power of Coincidence to Create Miracles.* Rider & Co. 2005.

Allen, Robert. G and Hansen, Mark Victor. *Cracking the Millionaire Code: Your Key to Enlightened Wealth.* Crown Business. 2005.

Canfield, Jack and Hansen, Mark. Victor. *Chicken Soup For The Soul: 101 Stories to Open the Heart and Rekindle the Spirit.* Westland. 2007

Dick, Dr. Frank W (OBE). *Winning: Motivation for Business Sport and Life.* 2006.

Deida, David . *Intimate Communion: Awakening Your Sexual Essence.* Health Communications, Inc. 1995.

Welch, Jack with Suzy. Welch. *Winning.* Harper Collins Publishers Ind Ltd. 2010

Brown, Les. *Live Your Dreams.* Harper Paperbacks. 1994.

Clason, George. S. *The Richest Man In Babylon.* Signet Book. 2008.

Robbins, Anthony. *Awaken The Giant Within: How to Take Immediate Control of Your Mental, Emotional, Physical and Financial Life.* Harper Collins Publishers. 2001.

Kiyosaki, Robert and Lechter, Sharon. L. *Rich Dad Poor Dad: What the Rich Teach their Kid about Money – That the Poor and Middle Class Do Not.* Warner Books. 2010.

Demartini, Dr John. F. *The Breakthrough Experience: A Revolutionary New Approach To Personal Transformation.* Hay House, Inc. 2002

Williams, Montel with Doyle, William. *Living Well: 21 Days to Transform your Life, Supercharge your health and feel spectacular.* New American Library. 2008.

Rohn, Jim. *7 Strategies For Wealth & Happiness.* Three Rivers Press (ca). 1996.

Eker, T. Harv. *Secrets Of The Millionaire Mind: Think Rich to Get Rich.* Harper Collins. 2005.

Schwartz, David. J. *The Magic of Thinking Big.* Pocket Books. 1995.

Twist, Lynne with Barker, Teresa. *The Soul of Money: Reclaiming the Wealth of Our Inner Resources.* W. W. Norton & Company. 2006.

The Foundation for Inner Peace. *A Course In Miracles.* Penguin U. K. 1997.

Proctor, Bob. *You Were Born Rich: Now you can discover and develop those riches.* 1997.

Bandler, Richard. *Magic In Action.* Meta Publications. 1992.

Wolfe, David. *Superfoods: The Food and Medicine of the Future.* North Atlantic Books. 2009.

Mandino, Og. *The Choice.* Bantam Books. 1984

Young, Robert. O and Young, Shelley. Redford. *The Ph Miracle: Balance Your Diet and Reclaim your Health.* Warner Books. 2002.

About the Author

For two decades, Rohan Weerasinghe has been speaking to audiences in the fields of education, inspiration, personal growth, business and wealth creation. The Bald Truth is a symbol of his honest, passionate and authentic style that holds no punches and delivers a powerful and life-changing message.

Having touched countless thousands of lives, Rohan is recognised as one of the UK's leading inspirational and wealth education speakers. He is sought-after globally to speak at corporate events, personal development and wealth conferences and has spoken for several major charities including Make-A-Wish, Peace One Day, MENCAP and Global Angels. Rohan is a regular speaker for Robert Kiyosaki's Rich Dad Education, one of the worlds largest wealth education companies.

At thirteen years of age, Rohan experienced the passing of his father. Inspired by his mother's determination to work two jobs whilst raising three sons alone, he focused on his academic education. He earned a PhD in Civil Engineering and later became one of the UK's leading consultants in his field. During this period Rohan nurtured his passion for helping others by speaking in schools, colleges, universities and companies, teaching personal development and growth.

After a series of personal life-challenges, Rohan created his own turning point and together with his friend and business associate, they developed a property portfolio that grew rapidly into a multi-million pound portfolio in just a few years. Also focussing on his health and relationship, he dramatically changed his life and was very soon being asked to share with others the tools and methods he used to create such a transformation.

Combining his engineering expertise with his vast experience in coaching and working with audiences, he created a form of "Human Engineering" that anybody can apply to re-stabilise their life and create new life-foundations. Ultimately what this life-technology does is enable rapid and impactful changes.

Rohan now runs several businesses, one of which provides coaching and mentoring for anyone looking to create significant personal and financial changes in their lives. He has helped people to overcome major health challenges, saved relationships, guided countless people on the path to financial independence, turned businesses around and created major turning points for people from all backgrounds and ages across the world.

Additional Programs, Products & Services to help you create Turning Points

A Personal Message

As part of my life purpose to inspire, educate and share tools that help people around the world to make powerful and lasting change, I continue to create a variety of products and services.

You will find many valuable free resources through my BLOG and Audio Podcasts at my website, where you can also register for a series of free newsletters covering subjects from Health to Wealth.

Visit: **www.thebaldtruth.co.uk** or **www.rohanlive.com**

Books, CD's & DVD's

Once you are registered with my website I will keep you posted on future books and educational programs. You may also enjoy the audio version of this book that has an additional self-hypnosis process to help reinforce your learning.

Other audio programs that I have specifically developed include creating wealth, massively improving your health and vitality and developing an even more amazing relationship. Look out for these on CD and also future DVD's.

Live Seminars

One of the most powerful ways to experience change and to rapidly produce positive and empowering Turning Points is when you immerse yourself in a live seminar. This is an area that I am truly passionate about. The seminars we run are designed to create lasting results and to re-align your vision, purpose and any area of your life that you choose to work on. The events are life changing and highly motivational. To find out when and where my next event is, visit the events page on the above websites.

The Bald Truth Coaching & Mentoring Program

One-to-one coaching and mentoring is one of the most effective ways to make positive changes in your life. If you would like to find out more about The Bald Truth coaching program, please register your interest through the email address below.

YouTube

By visiting and subscribing to my YouTube channel: RohansBaldTruth you will receive up-to-date educational and inspirational videos from around the world.

For any further enquiries simply visit our website or email: **enquiries@rohanlive.com**

Printed in Great Britain
by Amazon